Courage and *Confidence* *from* *the* **BIBLE**

by Walter L. Moore
and the
Editors of *Christian Herald*
with
the New American Library

foreword by Dr. Daniel A. Poling

a revised edition

A SPECIAL 1983 EDITION REISSUED BY THE CHRISTIAN HERALD ASSOCIATION

You Can Live A Happier Life

"Too many unfortunate people are dominated by insecurities that are gnawing away at their usefulness. What about yourself? Can you honestly say that your life is a happy one? If you cannot, would you like to say it and mean it? . . . It is for you, then, that this book has been prepared."

So says Dr. Daniel A. Poling, editor of the *Christian Herald,* and one of America's most noted churchmen, writers and civic leaders, in his introduction to this inspiring book.

Here you will find inspiring comfort and advice from the Bible. Included are short prayers and illuminating personal messages from Dr. Walter L. Moore, pastor of the First Baptist Church in Waycross, Georgia.

These meditations are categorized under headings of the most common anxieties troubling modern men and women. This invaluable book brings you friendly advice and inspiration to get you through these difficult times. It will show you how to overcome personal obstacles so you can lead a richer, happier life.

Table of Contents

Foreword

There is a need for a book of this kind. Too many unfortunate people are dominated by insecurities that are gnawing away at their usefulness. What about yourself? Can you honestly say that your life is a happy one? If you cannot, would you like to be able to say it and mean it? Are you perplexed because you do not seem to be getting ahead? Are you tortured by shame and guilt feelings that reach out of your past to taunt you? Do you feel lonely in a world that seems not to care whether you live or die? Are you making a success of your marriage?

As we seek here and there for answers to such vital problems as the above, looking for encouragement and strength and something sure upon which to pin our hopes, we sometimes forget the limitless resources of spiritual strength at our disposal. The root of most of our trouble is a lack of understanding. We do not understand ourselves, our fellow men, our relationship to the underlying forces of the universe. But in recent years more and more troubled souls are rediscovering for themselves the source book of understanding—the Bible.

Inner peace has been the subject of many books in the last decade, but the greatest of them all is a volume some two thousand years old. This Book that has outlasted kings and emperors, kingdoms and empires, tells how men and women over a broad span of time lived their lives for good or ill, conquered their fears and troubles or were conquered by them.

Some of our present-day conceptions of inner peace are grievously in error. Peace of mind, or peace of soul, or serenity of spirit is not a *do-nothing peace*. It is not a comfortable relaxation from the chores of life, nor a carefree recess from reality, nor a sheltered harbor where adverse winds never blow. Having true peace of mind does not mean that you will never face trouble. You will. Rain—and drought—come on the just and the unjust. Finding inner peace will not exempt you from the common hardships to which man is heir. *But it will make a tremendous difference in your facing up to those hardships!*

To be at peace in one's soul is not to be unmindful and uncaring of all the evils in the world which need righting. Inner peace is a *do-something* peace. It takes you not to a hermit's cave but to the office, the home, the club, the shop, the school, the legislature, and makes you a better, more alert, more sympathetic, more efficient, more magnetic personality. It does not close your eyes to world turmoil and human suffering, but gives you resources, poise, perspective for dealing confidently with them. This is the kind of peace the Bible offers and from which we may draw our strength.

And so it is not so startling after all that Isaiah, a man who wrote, "Thou wilt keep him in perfect peace, whose mind is stayed on thee," is reported by tradition to have been sawn asunder in the trunk of a tree at the order of a king we scarcely can recall. Nor that He who promised, "Peace I leave with you, my peace I give unto you," was crucified. His own inner peace did not keep Jesus from sorrowing over the sins of a city nor weeping at the grave of a friend. Not even the Master could deliver Himself from the cross; all He could do was transform it into the most heartening and healing and compassionate symbol the world has ever known!

And it is not so startling that within our own time, four chaplains—two Protestants, a Catholic, and a Jew—on a sinking troopship chose to give away their lifebelts to frightened lads who had none, and themselves go down with their ship, sustained only by their inner peace and their linked arms. A rescued engineer described the scene in these eloquent words: "They quieted the panic, forced men 'frozen' on the rail toward the boats and over the side, helped men adjust life jackets and at last gave away their own. They had no chance without them. I swam away from the ship and turned to watch. The flares now lighted everything. The bow came up high and she slid undei. The last I saw, the chaplains were up there praying for the safety of the men. They had done everything they could. I did not see them again."

Nor is it startling that a brilliant organist of Upper Alsace, the world's foremost authority on Johann Bach, student of Goethe and a great philosopher, left his applauding audiences, mastered a new profession after he had reached the age of thirty-four, and became a medical missionary. Albert Schweitzer has plumbed the secrets of happy living to greater depths than most, and his heart sent him to the rugged village of Lambaréné in French Equatorial Africa.

Inner peace *must* show itself in outward actions! If it does not, then religion is not an adventure, but an escape; and escapists will never change the world nor be happy with the portion of it they possess.

This little book comes to you, then, not primarily to make you feel good, but to feel good for something; not to deliver you from your handicaps, but to deliver you from yourself; not to tell you that you need face no obstacles, but to tell you that you may utilize your obstacles. And all these things must start first on the inside, down deep in your fretful, impatient, frustrated spirit.

HERE IS HELP FOR MEETING LIFE'S PERPLEXITIES

Today's living is so involved, so complex, that probably everyone has said at one time or another, "I wish I had someone to advise me on this—someone who really knows something about it." Many of our problems seem to have shifted from stark whites and blacks to muddled grays, because one problem in our life is not isolated but touches other problems. Our most difficult decisions lie at the intersection of the good with the better, and it is usually hard to know which is which. We move faster today than people used to move; even the rooster is swifter than his ancestor—if he gets across the road at all. We don't have as much time to make up our minds. When we hesitate a fraction of a second too long, the fellow in back of us blows his horn. Sometimes we feel farther from the end results of our problems than we should; we have delegated too much—our welfare services we have turned over to social agencies and our friendliness to the Welcome Wagon. And so it is harder to make a good decision when we may never see how our money or helping hand changes despair and loneliness into hope.

These are products of our age; some of them good, some of them undesirable, some of them harmful, most of them inescapable. But this is certain: our inner resources have not kept pace with our outer life. We haven't let our souls catch up with us. To do this, we need all the help we can get. We need any guidance that is well-informed. This book is that kind of guidance, because it comes from the greatest Answer Book of all time.

How can the Bible guide you today as you ponder a business deal or wave at your neighbor across the back fence? *By showing you how other folks solved their problems!* Even though today's tempo has speeded up, even though we ride in automobiles and subways instead of on beasts of burden, our underlying problems are just about the same—how to find security, how to be happy, how to be sure one's life is counting for something worth while. If you can learn such a secret from a man who wears sandals and a robe, it is easy enough to clothe him and his formula in shoes and a herringbone suit.

A woman drawing water from a well has nothing really important separating her from a woman turning the tap in a streamlined kitchen.

But not all the fascinating individuals who people the Guide Book are folks you would care to have as next-door neighbors, let alone hide them in your own personality. Some of them made mistakes—fearful mistakes. But you still need to become acquainted with these failures in the dark reaches of the past. Better to know about them and let *them* make *your* mistakes, than for you to fall into the same pit unawares. It is wasteful and many times quite unnecessary for you to make blunders that other people have already made, or to seek anxiously for a way out when others have found that way out. You may stand on the shoulders of the past—but only if you are acquainted with the past.

Apart from help through specific situations—the noble faith, for example, of Joseph, who resisted an enticing temptation to personal impurity; the stubborn faith of Job who trusted God when he had nothing left but trust; the reconsidering faith of Peter who usually spoke before he thought; the clean-cut faith of the young man with the godly grandmother, Timothy—apart from these, the Bible is a rich treasure house into which we may freely enter and bear away all that we can carry.

Who can read the beautiful Twenty-third Psalm that speaks of shepherds and still waters and shadowy valleys, and not be a better person? Who can shape the words of the fourteenth chapter of John's Gospel, shining words that have soothed sorrowing souls for nineteen centuries, and not look up more unafraid of death and life? Or who can listen to the story of how angels sang alleluias of peace in a troubled world, to a babe in a stable—and not lose some of his discouragement?

DR. MOORE'S BACKGROUND QUALIFIES HIM TO HELP OTHERS

Dr. Walter L. Moore, Pastor of the First Baptist Church of Waycross, Georgia, and author of these meditations, is a friendly, small-town man. *The Christian Herald* said of him: "In each of his pastorates, Dr. Moore has known almost everyone in town. And knowing people, to him, isn't merely knowing names and addresses; he has a 'sharing heart' which makes for real friendships." He is the kind of man who equally enjoys stopping on the street to ask his friends about their children, or reading his Greek New Testament. He knows something about farming, having been reared in an isolated rural section of Louisiana, and he has held such other jobs as Western Union messenger and bookkeeper while he was earning his way through school, later becoming a successful business executive. He left his promising commercial career to study for and enter the ministry.

Dr. Moore's wide cross section of experience, and his love for literature, God, and people have taught him how to make the Bible plain to folks who badly need its nuggets of faith and wisdom and courage. The little stories he has collected by his wide reading and his patient listening, light up the rich wealth of the Scriptures like a strong light behind stained glass. *The Christian Herald* has been fortunate to be able to share with its readers each month Dr. Moore's plain paragraphs on subjects that matter most. It is fitting that these heartening nuggets now be made available to many other thousands whose interests have been largely secular and who have had no close relationship with churches. We are all alike in our perplexities, and we all need to feel the steadying everlasting rock beneath our wavering feet.

THE MAGAZINE THAT WAS A
YOUNG MAN'S DREAM

The Christian Herald magazine itself represented the inner longings of one man as they found expression and embodiment. Louis Klopsch, though born in Germany, was essentially an American boy. His young life was spent in New York where he drifted from one enterprise to another. Always it was the new idea which appealed to him. He became interested in printing and publishing and was one of the pioneers of pictorial journalism, supplying newspapers with printing-plate portraits of men and women in the public eye. This business continued until the papers developed mechanical processes which enabled them to manufacture their own illustrations.

On a trip abroad, Mr. Klopsch made arrangements in England with the owner of *The Christian Herald* to take over the management of its American edition, and later he bought the paper outright. At the time, it had a circulation of thirty thousand, considered good for a religious journal. Mr. Klopsch announced that he would raise the circulation to a quarter of a million, and brought smiles to his associates. Before his death twenty years later, the paper had surpassed that figure, and today is the world's most powerful Protestant voice, with a readership of two million.

From its earliest days, *The Christian Herald* existed for a purpose: to help where help was needed. Russia, Armenia, India, China, Finland, Sweden, Japan, and Italy have been given aid in their times of poverty, famine, and calamity. Today, *The Christian Herald,* through its readers, supports an industrial school and two orphanages in China; Mont Lawn, a home at Nyack, New York, for children from New York City's under-privileged areas; the world-famed Bowery Mission on New York's sordid Skid Row; and the Memorial Home Community at Penney Farms, Florida, for retired Christian workers. The magazine's masthead today proclaims it "a family magazine, independent and interdenominational . . . dedicated to the promotion of evangelical Christianity, church unity, religious and racial understanding, world peace; the solving of the liquor problem, the service of the needy at home and abroad, and to cooperation with all who seek the establishment of a more Christian world."

All this because a young man once had a vision and set out to make it good.

A FEW SUGGESTIONS ON HOW
TO USE THIS BOOK

This is probably not the kind of book you will wish to sit down with and read at one sitting. You may read a single paragraph in a minute of time and be helped, but also these are "meditations," and more time is required for meditating; time for asking, when a finger of accusation is pointed, "Lord, is it I?" time to let the inspiration of soaring words stir your very being; time to let quieting words heal your troubled thoughts; time for the assurance of "Son, thy sins be forgiven thee" to lift your anxiety and tension. One does not undo the knots from a tangled soul in a moment, but even a moment can start the process.

You may wish to keep the book in a convenient place where you may pick it up during spare minutes—in the kitchen table drawer, the office desk, the dresser or bureau. Commuters will find it an excellent way in which to find inner rest and quiet even in the midst of hurry and confusion. The reading of this book will thus become a regular habit for many. There are 365 of these meditations—enough to undergird your thoughts every day for a year.

I think just now of the capable wood stove in our New Hampshire kitchen. The lower door had embossed upon it a legend in commanding letters: EMPTY ASHES DAILY. When the ashes were allowed to accumulate too long, the operation of that good stove was impaired. By the very process of living our lives, we accumulate ashes—little irritations and doubts and jealousies that sift down upon our souls—and these need to be lifted away. The meditation habit keeps your spirit clean, uncluttered, cleared for action. A few minutes a day spent with this book will open new channels by which the power of God may flow to you and through you.

Others will use it as a reference book. Are you troubled in a matter so personal that you find it difficult to discuss even with those who are closest to you? Are you too timid about your meager knowledge of religion and spiritual resources to go to a minister with your problem? Are some of your sorrows too deep for utterance? Then you will find the book immensely helpful as you match God's Word to your deepest need. One sentence, one verse, perhaps even a phrase or word, can change your life even as the lives of millions have been changed by whispers of the Divine.

Although each meditation is complete in itself, you will not avail yourself of the whole benefit of it unless you read also the Bible reference. And from that verse, you may wish to read on, discovering for yourself the broad highway and beckoning lanes that lead to challenging adventures for those who will follow and walk slowly, now and then to catch a breath of Heaven.

MY MESSAGE TO EACH AND EVERY ONE OF YOU

Be very sure that sometime, somewhere, you will be brought to a halt, by your own anchor imbedded deep in the open channel—or caught upon jagged rocks where you have been cast by wind and current. *It is important that you forge an anchor for yourself, and that your anchor hold.*

On a highway in France in February, 1918, I was glad that I had an anchor. I had just talked with a sick and fever-stricken young lieutenant, and he had stumbled on with his men. Then a three-inch shell came over and where there had been a man, breathing, speaking, walking, there was only blood, quivering flesh and muck. Had *he* suddenly disintegrated? Or was the real person living on? Stopped short, I had to face the question. God grant that you never see the horror of a battlefield. But still you will never finally escape this same agonizing question. Scream it aloud, sob out your *Why?* and *Where?* that men have hurled at the sky for so long the universe echoes with their despair. But know that the answer lies within your own heart and within the love that is in the world and must live on forever. Cast down your anchor there as I cast down mine.

And I was glad that I had that anchor when the troopship

Dorchester went down in the North Atlantic, for one of the four chaplains was my son.

You will find the eternal verities in the eternal Book—*and only there*. The Bible is the record of God's dealings with men, humble men for the most part, men with problems that kept them awake nights, men with doubts that ate into their hearts. The Bible shows what happens when God touches a man, a single individual. It is within one person that every great episode of history must begin. Dwight L. Moody, America's powerful and perhaps greatest evangelist, knew it and said, "The world has yet to see what God can accomplish with a man entirely yielded to him; and God willing, I will be that man!"

We have tried to anchor the world when we ourselves are not anchored. We have looked for the easy way out of problems and have looked everywhere but within ourselves. We speak of "push-button" warfare and act as if we believed in a "push-button" peace. But we may have nothing worth having without paying for it, because there are no "push-button" human souls. World peace, world security, world brotherhood, and friendliness must start in the heart of one person. You may be that one person. There can be no peace in the world unless there is peace in the heart of man. It is for you, then, that this book has been prepared. May it show you the way out of your fear and the path to peace with power which is God's waiting gift for you.

DANIEL A. POLING

Courage and Confidence
from the Bible

FEARS AND ANXIETY

Faith is the answer to your fear.

> But without faith it is impossible to please him: for he that cometh to God must believe that he is, and that he is a rewarder of them that diligently seek him. (Hebrews 11:6)

Faith is not a luxury, but a necessity of life. We must have faith in ourselves; the lack of it can paralyze us. We must have faith in the people around us or we shall be tortured with suspicion, jealousy, and fear. We must have faith in the processes of nature or we cannot live on the earth. But above all, we must have faith in the intelligence, good will, and dependability of Him in whose hands we live. Without faith it is impossible to please God, and without some sort of faith it is impossible to live.

⮿ Father, we have to believe in something. Save us from the folly of trusting that which is not trustworthy, and increase our faith in Thyself, who art true. Amen.

Do you fear because you fear to do?

> For when the Gentiles, which have not the law, do by nature the things contained in the law, these, having not the law, are a law unto themselves. (Romans 2:14)

No more solemn thought occurs to any of us than that we are accountable to God for our acts. His righteousness is beyond our understanding, but He assures us that we shall be judged according to the light we have. No man is left entirely without light concerning right and wrong. Conscience is not all-wise, but it is our guide. To say we should not follow it is to say we should do what we think is wrong.

⮿ For that within us which says, "I ought," we thank Thee, God, and ask for courage always to obey that voice. Amen.

And the worst monsters are only the smallest moths.

> And he said unto them, Why are ye so fearful? How is it that ye have no faith? (Mark 4:40)

A weird story by Edgar Allan Poe tells of a man lying on a lounge and seeing through the window a huge and terrible monster coming swiftly down the mountainside toward the house. Looking at the same place in the sunlight of the next day, he found that the monster was only a small death's-head moth crawling slowly down the window frame. Many of our fears have no more substance than that. Jesus told the disciples that their fear even in the face of real danger was evidence of a lack of faith.

Trusting ourselves in Thy hands, loving Father, we face the unknown future without fear. Amen.

An effective cure for your worries!

> Be careful for nothing; but in every thing by prayer and supplication with thanksgiving let your requests be made known unto God. (Philippians 4:6)

Worry, not work, kills people. John Wolcot in his *Expostulatory Odes* says, "Care to our coffin adds a nail, no doubt; and every grin, so merry, draws one out." Paul suggests an effective cure for worry: "Be careful for nothing." Certainly; but how keep from it? "In everything by prayer and supplication with thanksgiving let your requests be made known to God." Prayer is the antidote to worry.

Father, we would cast our cares on Thee this day, as Thou hast bidden us to do, knowing that Thou carest for us. Amen.

Why sleep with your worries?

> I will both lay me down in peace and sleep: for thou, Lord, only makest me dwell in safety. (Psalms 4:8)

From Leslie Weatherhead I got this suggestion: To determine your first thought in the morning, control what you think about at night. Having formed the habit of falling asleep worrying about problems and waking vaguely disturbed, I decided to try the experiment. For my last thought before sleeping I selected Isaiah 26:3: "Thou wilt keep him in perfect peace, whose mind is stayed on thee . . ." Without too much difficulty I managed to keep turning the words over in my mind until I fell asleep. It worked. My text was the first thought in my mind next morning. It has also worked with other texts. Try it sometime.

Teach us, dear God, to hide Thy word in our hearts, that we may not sin against Thee, even by worrying. Amen.

Do you wish your burden were lightened?

> And it came to pass, that, as he was praying in a certain place, when he ceased, one of his disciples said unto him, Lord, teach us to pray, as John also taught his disciples. (Luke 11:1)

The prayer life of Jesus so impressed His disciples that the one thing they asked Him to teach them was to pray. Yet not all of His petitions were granted, for the time came when He said, "Not as I will, but as Thou wilt." But even from Gethsemane He went out prepared for Calvary. William Mountford says: "There is no burden of the spirit but is lightened by kneeling under it." Little by little the bitterest feelings are sweetened by the mention of them in prayer. And agony itself stops swelling, if we can only cry sincerely, "My God, my God!"

Our prayer is by Augustine: "Give me Thine own self, without whom, though Thou shouldest give all that ever Thou made, yet could not my desires be satisfied." Amen.

You have peace of mind within your own grasp.

> If ye then, being evil, know how to give good gifts unto your children, how much more shall your Father which is in heaven give good things to them that ask him? (Matthew 7:11)

A man made a long trip to ask a trusted minister friend to pray for him and his family. "Have *you* prayed about your troubles?" asked the pastor. "No," was the surprising answer. "I'm no good at that sort of thing." "You are unfair to God," the minister told him. "How would you feel if your small son would not talk with you about his troubles, but asked a schoolmate to beg you to help him?"

Confidently we come to Thee, dear Father, not because we are skilled in prayer, but because Thou art loving and understanding. We trust ourselves to Thee. Amen.

And modern science tells you exactly the same thing.

> Ask, and it shall be given you; seek, and ye shall find; knock, and it shall be opened unto you. (Matthew 7:7)

Dr. T. Bulkley told the British Medical Association: "As an alienist, and one whose whole life has been concerned with sufferings of the mind, I would state that of all the hygienic measures to counteract disturbed sleep, depression of the spirits, and all the miserable sequels of a disturbed mind, I would undoubtedly give the first place to the simple habit of prayer." Paul said: "Let your requests be made known unto God. And the peace of God . . . shall keep your hearts."

Grateful for Thy blessings, and most of all for Thyself, we open our hearts to Thee, O God, that Thou mayest fill them with Thy peace. Amen.

Here's one always to remember!

> And he made a porch of pillars; the length thereof was fifty cubits, and the breadth thereof thirty cubits: and the porch was before them: and the other pillars and the thick beam were before them. (I Kings 7:6)

The army of Benhadad which invaded Palestine in Elisha's day dealt with the Israelitish forces easily, but when they imagined they heard great hosts approaching, which they could not see, they fled in panic. Imaginary enemies were more powerful than real ones. They usually are. A doctor says: "People's minds give me more trouble than their bodies. It is far easier to deal with the prosaic ills they have than the fantastic ones they imagine they have." Jesus always dealt with the mental side of every afflicted person by reassurance: "Be of good cheer. Fear not. Thy faith hath made thee whole."

We accept this day of life as from Thy gracious hand, dear Lord, assured that Thy love has prompted everything it may bring. Amen.

You will know better where you are when you discover where you are going.

> And we know that all things work together for good to them that love God, to them who are the called according to his purpose. (Romans 8:28)

Watching the workman, I almost thought he was confused, until I learned that he was not building a table, as I had supposed, but rather a bookshelf. Mistaking his purpose, I could see no reason for his actions. So it is difficult for us to see that "all things work together for good to them that love God, to them who are called according to his purpose," until we discover that His purpose is that they may be "conformed to the image of his Son." The thorn, the lash, and the cross are necessary sculptor's tools to fashion the image.

O Thou sculptor of souls, we rejoice that Thou hast seen in us material that can be made into Christ's image. Do to us whatever will make us more like Him. Amen.

Life comes in breaths, not years.

> Take therefore no thought for the morrow: for the morrow shall take thought for the things of itself. (Matthew 6:34)

Jesus taught the important lesson that life should be lived one day at a time. The Alcoholics Anonymous help those who are battling against alcoholism to win victory by staying sober for one day at a time. An elderly woman who had suffered a multiple hip fracture asked her doctor: "How long must I stay in bed?" His answer: "One day at a time." Daily bread and daily grace are given to us for one day at a time.

Our Father which art in heaven, give us this day our daily bread and our daily measure of grace. Amen.

Tomorrow's troubles are always the most fearful.

> Trust in the Lord, and do good; so shalt thou dwell in the land, and verily thou shalt be fed. (Psalms 37:3)

A philosopher of the homespun school remarked, "I've had a great deal of trouble in my life." After a pause he added, "Most of it never happened." Weymouth translates Jesus' warning against the folly of borrowing trouble from tomorrow: "Do not be anxious, therefore, about tomorrow, for tomorrow will bring its own anxieties. Enough for each day is its own trouble."

Father, we would be so diligent about today's duties, and so confident of Thy care, that we shall have neither time nor disposition to be anxious about tomorrow. Amen.

One way to get rid of your fears.

> Casting all your care upon him, for he careth for you. (I Peter 5:7)

Years ago a good old bishop was tossing in his bed at midnight, worrying his heart over what seemed to him the evils of a doomed world, when he thought he heard the Lord say: "Go to sleep, Bishop. I'll sit up the rest of the night." Serious-minded people can find much to worry about now, and it sometimes seems that the clock has stopped at midnight. But we shall do well to remember that God has not gone to sleep.

✿ *God of Thy troubled people, who sometimes feel that their way is passed over by Thee, open our eyes that we may see Thee watching and working in Thy world. Amen.*

Spend today wisely.

> . . . Where hast thou gleaned to day? and where wrought-est thou? blessed be he that did take knowledge of thee . . . (Ruth 2:19)

For Naomi and Ruth the past was tragic, the future uncertain. But the question at evening was: "Where hast thou gleaned today?" Life is lived fruitfully one day at a time. Our Lord taught us to pray for one day's bread. It is vain to regret or boast of the past. Worry over the future is harmful. We must "act in the living present." Yesterday is a canceled check; tomorrow is a promissory note; only today is cash in hand, and it should be spent wisely.

✿ *Give us this day bread, strength, courage, and light sufficient for the day's needs, and wisdom to live each day at its best. Amen.*

Two things you should never worry about:

> Wait on the Lord: be of good courage, and he shall strengthen thine heart . . . (Psalms 27:14)

Dr. Reinhold Niebuhr has written a prayer which so well expresses our constant need that it has been widely quoted: "God grant me the serenity to accept the things I cannot change; the courage to change the things I can; and the wisdom to know the difference." A homespun philosopher has said: "There are two things about which we should never worry: the things we can't help and the things we can." The courage to tackle a situation that can be remedied and the patience to endure that which is beyond our control are but two expressions of the Christian spirit.

✿ *O Thou source of all wisdom and strength, teach us to meet life's duties and disciplines in the spirit of Jesus. Amen.*

Some of our worst moments are caused by—ourselves.

> . . . so fight I, not as one that beateth the air: But I keep under my body, and bring it into subjection . . . (I Corinthians 9:26, 27)

Some time ago, a full-length mirror in a Venice, California, ballroom was smashed and a young man suffered severe cuts on his right hand. Arrested on a charge of intoxication, the wounded fighter indignantly insisted that he had walked into the room and had seen the "other guy" looking at him "very nasty." Most of us carry on a much more serious and sober battle with ourselves constantly. Paul said: "So fight I, not as one that beateth the air: But I keep under my body, and bring it into subjection."

Thou who knowest the battles we fight, give us courage and strength to overcome the enemies within our own souls. Amen.

When you don't know which end's up, do this:

> But the God of all grace, who hath called us unto his eternal glory by Christ Jesus, after that ye have suffered a while, make you perfect, stablish, strengthen, settle you. (I Peter 5:10)

Long ago I learned that when I become a bit seasick, by laying my head back and closing my eyes, I can regain my sense of equilibrium. This has been worth a great deal to me many times, when the sea was disturbed or when the air was rough for a plane trip. But a greater discovery has been the stabilizing effect of prayer. When moorings slip and we are in danger of losing our sense of values or direction, talking with God about it will straighten us out. A sign outside a chapel in Sheffield, England, had it this way: "If you don't know whether you're on your head or your heels, get on your knees."

We come to Thee, Thou unchanging God, to set our compasses true for life's voyage. Amen.

You have more faith than you think.

> For the Lord shall be thy confidence, and shall keep thy foot from being taken. (Proverbs 3:26)

Even the simplest activities of life require some faith. We must believe that our senses are dependable and our minds rational. We have to trust our universe, assuming that the sun will rise tomorrow, the seasons follow each other, the processes of biochemistry continue. Science must take it for granted that the universe makes sense and that its operation is consistent. We live by faith or are paralyzed. So faith is essential for living as spiritual beings. Believing in righteousness, love, and wisdom as being of the very nature of God, we can live confidently as His children.

🙞 *We commit our ways unto Thee, O Lord. Help us to build our lives on faith in Thy character. In Jesus' name we pray. Amen.*

Fear can never be conquered by pampering.

And when they had preached the gospel to that city, and had taught many, they returned again to Lystra, and to Iconium, and Antioch, Confirming the souls of the disciples, and exhorting them to continue in the faith, and that we must through much tribulation enter into the kingdom of God. (The Acts 14:21, 22)

At Lystra, Paul met the most violent opposition, which culminated in his being stoned, dragged outside the city, and left for dead. Revived, he went on to Derbe. One would think that, having escaped from Lystra, he would have stayed away. But he knew that his converts there would have to face persecution, and he who had been through it was the one best qualified to prepare them to endure it. So back he went to encourage them to be steadfast.

🙞 *We do not pray for a safe and easy life, God of the martyrs, but for the spirit which considers Thy kingdom first, and personal welfare not at all. Amen.*

Listen for the stranger's song.

Who being past feeling have given themselves over unto lasciviousness, to work all uncleanness with greediness. (Ephesians 4:19)

On a lonely, backwoods road my car stalled, and I had to leave my wife and baby to go for help. It was growing dark, and she was afraid. Soon she saw the figure of a man approaching in the gloom. Her heart stood still. Would he molest them? Her panic increased as he drew nearer. Then she heard something that quieted all her fears. He was whistling a familiar tune: "Where He Leads Me I Will Follow." People who sing hymns when alone can usually be trusted, for songs come from the heart.

🙝 *O Thou of whom the Psalmists sang, we thank Thee for the great hymns of the Church. Teach us to share the faith and commitment they express. Amen.*

There's a mixture of courage and fear in all of us.

> . . . Be strong and of a good courage; be not afraid, neither be thou dismayed: for the Lord thy God is with thee whithersoever thou goest. (Joshua 1:9)

Courage is not all of one piece. One may be unmoved by great physical danger and frightened at a banquet. He may be irresistible in battle and yet surrender ignobly to moral temptation. Some of us are occasionally involved in situations that require physical courage, but all of us are constantly in need of moral courage. To stand for the right when it is unpopular, to be faithful to duty when your heart is broken, to be a Christian in a pagan world—these take courage.

🙝 *O Thou who givest strength to the faint, we would be brave in the unusual times of physical danger, but oh, give us stout hearts to meet the constant tests of our moral courage. Amen.*

Do you seek God only when you must?

> Jesus said unto him, Thou shalt love the Lord thy God with all thy heart, and with all thy soul, and with all thy mind. (Matthew 22:37)

A young woman walking by a church on a weekday noticed a little girl coming out of the sanctuary. Seeking to engage the child in conversation, she asked, "Where have you been, my dear?" "In there." "And what were you doing in there?" "Just praying." Thinking that perhaps the child was troubled about something, she inquired, "What did you ask God for, dear?" "Oh, nothing; I was just loving God a little."

🙝 *Our Father which art in heaven, hallowed be Thy name. Amen.*

FAILURE IN GETTING AHEAD—RIVALRY

You can't expect to be boss this afternoon.

> And in the eleventh year . . . was the house finished throughout all the parts thereof, and according to all the fashion of it. So was he seven years in building it. (I Kings 6:38)

Seven years were required for Solomon to build the temple, one of the most magnificent structures ever built. Great and important accomplishments require time and patience. Bryant rewrote his *Thanatopsis* a hundred times and even then was not satisfied with it. Gibbon worked for twenty years to produce *The Decline and Fall of the Roman Empire*. Butler wrote his famous *Analogy* twenty times. Virgil took seven years to write his *Georgics*, and twelve to produce the *Aeneid*. "Let us not be weary in well doing, for in due season we shall reap, if we faint not."

Father, we thank Thee for tasks that are worthy of years of effort. Keep us faithful to them. Amen.

Do you spend too much time on shingles?

> . . . behold, a man turned aside, and brought a man unto me, and said, Keep this man: if by any means he be missing, then shall thy life be for his life . . . And as thy servant was busy here and there, he was gone . . . And he said unto him, Thus saith the Lord, Because thou hast let go out of thy hand a man whom I appointed to utter destruction, therefore thy life shall go for his life, and thy people for his people. (I Kings 20:39, 40, 42)

An artist was out one day with his pupils, sketching. One young man was engaged in sketching a landscape bathed in the soft light of the setting sun. In the foreground was a large barn. The teacher watched the young man quietly for a while and then said to him, "If you spend so much time in painting the shingles on that barn, you will not have time to paint the sunset. You will have to choose between the two." Frequently we discover that a sunset has faded while we have been painting shingles. Busy here and there, we have let glorious opportunities escape us.

We do not ask, Father, to be able to recover our lost opportunities, but we seek Thy help that we may choose wisely that at which we will spend our time in the year ahead. Amen.

To get going, you have to start.

> I press toward the mark for the prize of the high calling of
> God in Christ Jesus. (Philippians 3:14)

The crime of which many of us are guilty is not "low aim,"
but "no aim." A homespun philosopher observes that "the reason some people don't get nowhere is that they didn't start nowhere in the first place." A writer in *Forbes Magazine* tells of
a little boy he met trudging along a country road with a cat-
rifle over his shoulder. "What are you hunting, Buddy?" he
asked. "Dunno, sir," was the reply. "I ain't seen it yet." Life
can be great only when it has a great goal. In Christ, Paul
found a goal that challenged and thrilled him.

*We dedicate ourselves anew to Thee, O Christ, as the
goal of our lives, the guide for each day, and the source of
strength for our striving. Amen.*

Don't forget to do the little things.

> For who hath despised the day of small things? . . . (Zech-
> ariah 4:10)

The chemical composition of a great mass is determined by
an analysis of a tiny portion of it. So the quality of a long life
is seen in little daily acts. Such things as giving a cup of cold
water or visiting an unfortunate brother will decide our eternal destiny, according to Jesus. Such trivial things as little
courtesies, little kindnesses, pleasant words, friendly letters,
good wishes, and kind deeds make up a gracious life. "Do little
things now," says a Persian proverb, "so shall big things come
to thee by and by, asking to be done."

*Help us, Lord Jesus, to be so suffused with Thy spirit
that Thou mayest be discovered in every tiniest segment of
our lives. Amen.*

There are no loose ends on the way to advancement.

> I must work the works of him that sent me, while it is day:
> the night cometh, when no man can work. (John 9:4)

A useful lesson for effective living is: finish each task and
don't leave loose ends to be picked up later. A famous and re-
markably useful woman said recently, in an address to a group
of college students: "I try to make it a rule never to pick up
a paper on my desk twice. If possible, I dispose of it at once."

She is able to do a tremendous amount of work largely because of that one habit.

❧ Help us, O Thou working God, to live today at its best and, as far as possible, greet the evening with the day's tasks done. Amen.

Have you dignified your job by believing in it?

> Is not this the carpenter . . . ? And they were offended at him (Mark 6:3)

The neighbors of Jesus were wrong in thinking that because He was a carpenter He could not be the Christ. He was no less the Son of God when making an easy yoke than when teaching a lesson about it. He said, "My Father worketh hitherto, and I work." Tolstoy tells in one of his stories of a Crimean peasant who, when forced to plow on Easter day, lighted a votive candle and attached it to his plow. So, as he followed the furrow back and forth throughout the sacred day, his labor became a sacrament. All who do honest, useful toil may feel that He is near.

❧ O Thou great workman, we here and now dedicate this day's labor to Thee. Use what we do to bless others of Thy children, our brothers and sisters. Amen.

Do you worry over a missed opportunity?

> . . . but this one thing I do, forgetting those things which are behind, and reaching forth unto those things which are before. (Philippians 3:13)

Bobby Jones, hero of the fabulous "grand slam" in golf, is quoted as having said that the most important lesson to learn in the game that made him famous is that "the ball must be played from where it lies." Worry over a poor stroke, or exultation over a particularly good one, can be equally disastrous. The most important stroke of the match is the one you are about to make. To be a champion one must learn to concentrate on the thing at hand. Paul said: "Forgetting those things which are behind, and reaching forth unto those things which are before, I press toward the mark."

❧ Lord of our lives, we thank Thee for each new unmarred day. Help us live today at its best, however poor our use of yesterday. Amen.

Can you keep on when keeping on is tiresome?

> And he reared up the court round about the tabernacle and the altar, and set up the hanging of the court gate. So Moses finished the work. (Exodus 40:33)

The thrill about starting on any great venture necessarily fades into monotony in carrying on. For Moses to build the tabernacle in the wilderness was a great undertaking. It began with a mountaintop experience of visions and revelations. It required organization, planning, constant overseeing, and perseverance. Some details were perhaps neglected or deferred. But there was no letup until it could be said: "So Moses finished the work."

Saviour, who didst say of Thine own work, "It is finished," keep us faithful to every good work until we can echo Thy words. Amen.

Think of the dinosaur!

> This is the word of the Lord . . . Not by might, nor by power, but by my spirit, saith the Lord of hosts. (Zechariah 4:6)

The skeletons of prehistoric monsters indicate that some of these beasts were more powerful than any of those that survived them. They perished not for lack of strength, but for lack of judgment. They were unable to adjust themselves to the immutable laws of life. So empires and civilizations disappear, not for lack of physical resources, but by violating God's laws! The future belongs to the people who adjust themselves to the facts. The greatest fact is God.

God of the nations, we pray that our country may become strong, not merely in physical force, but in the righteousness of her course. Amen.

Aim, more than advantage, is what counts.

> And having this confidence, I know that I shall abide and continue with you all for your furtherance and joy of faith. (Philippians 1:25)

Horace Mann, educator and statesman, was born over 150 years ago in such poverty that until he was fifteen he was never able to attend school for more than eight or ten weeks during any year. His most effective teacher was the pastor of his little village church. At twenty, he fell in with a good college preparatory teacher and in six months fitted himself for admission to the sophomore class of Brown University. He went on to become one of the great leaders of education in Massachusetts and the nation. Two men, a pastor and a teacher, gave him the necessary vision. His last words to his students were: "Be ashamed to die until you have won some victory for humanity."

God, bless the pastors and teachers and all others who inspire young people to strive for the heights. Amen.

The toughest jobs offer the greatest satisfactions.

> For a great door and effectual is opened unto me, and there are many adversaries. (I Corinthians 16:9)

Paul planned to remain at Ephesus because a great and effectual door was opened unto him, and there were many adversaries. Opportunity and opposition came together. They usually do. An unknown philosopher has remarked: "The trouble with opportunity is that it always comes disguised as hard work." An army never wins a victory until it meets the enemy. A hero is not he who loves the safe and easy place, but he who seeks the thickest of the fray. Paul, hero for God, would not leave, because he had found a hard, worthwhile job.

Forgive us, Father, our love of ease, and give us the thrill of doing things that challenge us to our best. Amen.

Unhappy is the man who scatters his shots.

> And Elijah came unto all the people, and said, How long halt ye between two opinions? if the Lord be God, follow him: but if Baal, then follow him . . . (I Kings 18:21)

A rifle bullet will penetrate far deeper than a pellet from a shotgun shell, though the scatter gun fires a heavier load. The difference is that all of the energy of the rifle cartridge is focused on one point of impact, while the shotgun wastes its force trying to cover a large area. Some lives, like birdshot, are spread out too wide to have much force. The trouble is not that those concerned have decided on the wrong course, but that they have never really decided on any course.

Thou hast given to us the Godlike power to choose. Give us courage to make the right choices. For Jesus' sake. Amen.

Are you part of an important task?

> For who hath despised the day of small things? . . . they are the eyes of the Lord, which run to and fro through the whole earth. (Zechariah 4:10)

Zechariah's question was suggested by the modest beginnings made toward rebuilding the temple at Jerusalem. To those who could see only the few stones laid, the work was insignificant. But he who could see the working out of the purposes of God saw a mighty movement under way. The importance of anything is determined not by what it is, but by what it is becoming. To be truly significant, our lives must be linked to the causes and institutions that are destined to greatness.

Father, we thank Thee for babies that can become men and women, and for humble beginnings that can change the world. Guide us to choose wisely the things to which we link our lives. Amen.

Do you put "zing" into your routine tasks?

> Whatsoever thy hand findeth to do, do it with thy might . . . (Ecclesiastes 9:10)

The ancient sage gives needed advice. If you are brushing your teeth, hoeing the garden, visiting the sick, or driving a nail, put some "zing" into it. Make an adventure of it. There is no reason why today should not be one of the most interesting days of your life. The thing you must do has some very interesting features. Get the most out of it by putting yourself into it.

Father, we thank Thee for the endless variety and surprises of living. Help us to make today thrilling by meeting it on tiptoe. Amen.

You may be more important than you think.

> But even the very hairs of your head are all numbered. Fear not therefore: ye are of more value than many sparrows. (Luke 12:7)

Jesus never tried to make anyone feel small. Rather, He was constantly reassuring people as to their real importance. Little children were not to be rebuffed, for "of such is the kingdom of heaven." Women were honored as persons, never despised. Young people were challenged to high heroism, the sick and afflicted were ministered to, sinners were forgiven and re-claimed. He insisted that all might face the future confident of God's careful attention, for "ye are of more value than many sparrows." You, He told us, are more important than you think you are.

✒ Father God, who carest for even the little bird, help all the little people of the world to see how important they are in Thy loving sight. We ask it in Jesus' name. Amen.

Successful men are always road builders.

> Jesus said unto him, If thou canst believe, all things are possible to him that believeth. (Mark 9:23)

A certain society in South Africa, it is said, wrote to David Livingstone: "Have you found a good road to where you are? If so, we want to know how to send other men to join you." Livingstone replied: "If you have men who will come only if they know there is a good road, I don't want them. I want men who will come if there is no road." The work of Christ is never easy. His need is not for followers who will do the easy or obvious thing, but for those who will do the impossible for His sake.

✒ Almighty Father, we believe that in Thy strength we can do anything that ought to be done. In that faith, we commit our lives anew to Thy service. Amen.

Wait for the big job, and you may wait a long time.

> As they ministered to the Lord, and fasted, the Holy Ghost said, Separate me Barnabas and Saul for the work where-unto I have called them. (The Acts 13:2)

Barnabas and Saul were selected to be foreign missionaries after they had distinguished themselves as workers in the An-tioch church. The test of loyalty and the qualification for greater responsibility is not what one thinks he would do were he in a great place, but rather it is one's everyday faith-fulness where he is. In the parable of the talents, those who were made rulers over many things were the ones who had been faithful over a few things.

✒ Wise Master, teach us to see the possibilities in our pres-ent situation and the greatness of faithfulness in little things. Amen.

What you thought were blessings may be ballast.

> . . . let us lay aside every weight, and the sin which doth so easily beset us, and let us run with patience the race that is set before us. (Hebrews 12:1)

Admiral Byrd, on one of his expeditions to the South Pole, observed that the load of his plane was too heavy to cross a lofty mountain range directly ahead. He commanded the trap doors to be opened and cases of canned goods to be pushed out into space. There was nothing wrong with the supplies but, by sacrificing them, sufficient altitude could be gained to clear the mountains. For the highest attainment in any realm, other things, perfectly legitimate in themselves, must be sacrificed.

Teach us, O God, what things are most worthwhile in our lives and what things are ballast that ought to go overboard. Amen.

No successful man ever despised his vocation.

> Jesus saith unto them, My meat is to do the will of him that sent me, and to finish his work. (John 4:34)

Charles M. Schwab is quoted as having said that a man who does not work for love of the work, but only for money, is not likely to make money or find much fun in life. Some unfortunate people live without working; others, equally unfortunate, work without living. Happy are those who really live in and through their work! In doing the work of His Father by leading the Samaritan woman to a knowledge of eternal truth, Jesus experienced a thrill that all the play in the world could not have equaled.

Teach us to see our work in the light of the Father's will, dear Master, and make it for us an offering to Him. Amen.

Into which of the three parts do you fit?

> And before him shall be gathered all nations: and he shall separate them one from another, as a shepherd divideth his sheep from the goats. (Matthew 25:32)

Charles Kingsley once wrote a letter to the young men of his congregation in which he said: "My dear young men: The human race may, for practical purposes, be divided into three parts—honest men who mean to do right and do it; knaves

who mean to do wrong and do it; fools who mean to do which-
ever of the two is pleasanter. And these last may be divided
into black fools and white fools—black fools who would
rather do wrong than right, but dare not unless it is the fashion; white fools who would rather do right than wrong, but
dare not unless it is the fashion."

*O Thou courageous Christ, who didst tread the winepress
alone, and who dost challenge us to take a cross and follow
Thee, help us to be worthy of Thee, our leader. Amen.*

Be thankful if you are discontented with your lot.

> . . . for every one that exalteth himself shall be abased;
> and he that humbleth himself shall be exalted. (Luke 18:14)

To Jesus the only hopeless cases were the people who were
satisfied with themselves. A sinner standing afar off and begging abjectly for mercy was better off than the Pharisee conscious of no need. Penitent prostitutes and publicans would
enter His kingdom ahead of self-righteous churchmen. The
greatest life tragedy was not to fall, but to lie there. An old
boatman was asked: "If a man fell into the waters here,
would he drown?" He answered: "No, it's not falling into
water that drowns a man; it's staying there."

*Save us, O Christ, from aims so low that we shall become
satisfied with ourselves. Amen.*

Not power, but how you use it, is the yardstick.

> And they were all amazed, and spake among themselves,
> saying, What a word is this! for with authority and power
> he commandeth the unclean spirits, and they come out.
> (Luke 4:36)

Jesus and Alexander the Great, each of whom lived for only
thirty-three years, were both men of unusual powers. Alexander conquered nations, but was unable to rule himself.
Jesus did many wondrous works of mercy. Today, Jesus is
worshipped and Alexander is pitied. The difference is not
merely in the power each possessed, but in the use made of it.
The test of greatness is not in the strength one has, but in the
cause to which one gives one's strength.

*Make us great, O God, not in the amount of strength we
have, but in the use of the powers we are given. Amen.*

Were you ever thankful for having work to do?

> And the Lord God took the man, and put him into the garden of Eden to dress it and to keep it. . . . Six days shalt thou labour, and do all thy work. (Genesis 2:15; Exodus 20:9)

We are told in the creation story that God made man, and put him into the Garden of Eden to care for and keep it. Work, then, did not originate as a punishment for sin, but was one of the pleasures of paradise. The curse was a wrong attitude toward work, and this continues unabated. The idea that loafing is living is a widespread modern heresy. There is no finer satisfaction than to do one's share of the world's work. It is one's way of serving, of being useful to God and one's fellows, and the most effective anesthetic for sorrow. When God was born of woman, He became a working man.

❧ *Heavenly Father, we thank Thee for the work we have to do. Help us to do it always as service to Thee. In Jesus' name. Amen.*

"Flash in the pan," photographers call it:

> And let us not be weary in well doing: for in due season we shall reap, if we faint not. (Galatians 6:9)

On my desk is a carton of flash bulbs, but I must go out and buy a bulb for my reading lamp. The flash bulb makes a light many times as bright as the ordinary incandescent lamp, but it does not last long enough to read by. Steadiness and dependability are more important in a reading lamp than exceptional brilliance. So it is with Christian lives. The people who are the light of the world are not brilliant flashes, but steady lamps.

❧ *We thank Thee, O God, for the reading-lamp Christians whose lives burn steadily. Make us like them. Amen.*

Not how fast, but how well did you do the job?

> . . . he that giveth, let him do it with simplicity; he that ruleth, with diligence; he that sheweth mercy, with cheerfulness. (Romans 12:8)

Happy is he who has learned to make each task of the day a small adventure. One of the best ways is to try to do each thing as well as possible. We never become bored by working at a masterpiece. One of the happiest men I know is janitor at a post office. He takes great pride in having the cleanest, loveliest little post-office building in the land.

🙡 *O Thou carpenter of Galilee, we pray Thy blessing upon all who work. Teach us to have joy and pride in our tasks. Amen.*

Three keys to solving problems on the job:

> And suddenly there came a sound from heaven as of a rushing mighty wind . . .
> And there appeared unto them cloven tongues like as of fire, and it sat upon each of them. (The Acts 2:2, 3)

A neon sign in front of an electric power company office rhythmically flashes these words: "Light, heat, power." They are the three words that move men to action. The light of knowledge and understanding must come first; then the warmth of feeling; and finally the power of will to act. When the Holy Spirit came upon the Church at Pentecost, the flaming tongues of fire represented light and heat, and the rushing mighty wind meant power. He enlightens our understanding of Christ, warms our hearts to love Him, and empowers our wills to serve Him.

🙡 *Spirit of God, come Thou upon us to give light for our darkness, warmth for our coldness, and power for our weakness. For Jesus' sake. Amen.*

RESTLESSNESS

Use your time wisely.

> And he said unto them, Come ye yourselves apart into a desert place, and rest a while: for there were many coming and going, and they had no leisure so much as to eat. (Mark 6:31)

Jesus, the busiest man who ever lived, was also a leisurely individual. He had time for people, time for prayer, time to observe and meditate. When Jesus left His disciples, He told them to tarry until they should be imbued with power. God has given us enough time for the essentials. Let us take time to do our work well, to relax and rest, to be with loved ones, and to worship and serve our Father. Learning to live is largely a matter of using time wisely.

❧ *God of the eternal ages, forgive our anxious restlessness, and teach us to relax in Thee. Amen.*

Whoa, there! Take it easy.

> But let patience have her perfect work, that ye may be perfect and entire, wanting nothing. (James 1:4)

Patience is a rare achievement, but essential for happy and effective living. Mohammed used to say that patience is the key to contentment. God has many methods of teaching His children patience, and the most successful one is to send trouble upon them. Paul observed that "tribulation worketh patience," and James agreed that "the trying of your faith worketh patience." But he added, "Let patience have her perfect work, that ye may be perfect and entire, wanting nothing."

❧ *Father, who art always patient with us, we thank Thee for life's discipline. Help us to learn the lessons our trials have to teach us. Amen.*

Does silence frighten you, or does it renew your mind?

> Be still, and know that I am God . . . (Psalms 46:10)

In a sermon on the "Significance of Silence," Leslie Weatherhead reminds us that most of the occasions when our souls are stirred most deeply are marked by silence. Profound grief is often speechless, and so is great worship. Of such an experience he says: "You know that God was near, that He was speaking to you, that He brought you to that hour and to that place in order to say things to you in silence that otherwise you would not have stayed to hear."

~ *O Thou who dost come to us in the voice of stillness, quiet our hearts, and teach us to be still and know that Thou art God. Amen.*

Minutes that give you strength:

> And in the morning, rising up a great while before day, he went out, and departed into a solitary place, and there prayed. (Mark 1:35)

Simon and his friends knew where to look for Jesus when they awoke and found Him gone from His bedroom. He had slipped out in the crisp freshness of the morning for a little time of unhurried fellowship with His Father. The day was to be a busy one, and He felt the need of spiritual preparation for it. It is a good rule to make prayer the key to every day and the lock to each night. Let us linger with God before entering upon our tasks!

~ *O Thou who didst commune with Jesus in the Galilean dawn, come and prepare us to walk this day and this year in His steps. Amen.*

Quiet words about the greatest Power of all:

> . . . In returning and rest shall ye be saved; in quietness and in confidence shall be your strength . . . (Isaiah 30:15)

In the Bible, reference is frequently made to the value of quietness for the spirit. "In quietness and in confidence shall ye be saved." "They that wait upon the Lord shall renew their strength." "Be silent, O all flesh, before the Lord." "Be still, and know that I am God." So now: "Be still and listen, the Master speaks to thee; be still and listen, He speaks so tenderly. He speaks in the morning freshness, He speaks in the noonday glow, He speaks in the quiet of evening. Be still, and then you'll know."

~ *God of the still, small voice, teach us to be quiet before Thee. Amen.*

You won't win wisdom at seventy miles an hour.

> Wait on the Lord: be of good courage, and he shall strengthen thine heart: wait, I say, on the Lord. (Psalms 27:14)

F. B. Meyer wrote: "The Bible seldom speaks, and certainly never its deepest, sweetest words, to those who always read in a hurry. Nature can only tell her secrets to such as will sit in her sacred temple till their eyes lose the glare of earthly glory and their ears are attuned to her voice. And shall revelation do what Nature cannot? Never! The man who shall win the blessedness of hearing the voice of divine wisdom must watch daily at the gates."

Though this moment of meditation be brief, Master, may it not be hurried. Give us Thy timeless patience and peace. Amen.

This is the haven for your restless soul.

> Commit thy way unto the Lord; trust also in him; and he shall bring it to pass. (Psalms 37:5)

John Marvin Rast tells in his syndicated column that Horace Bushnell awoke one morning with a consciousness of spiritual power such as he had never known before. His wife, noticing the change, asked him what had happened. "The gospel!" he answered. Later he explained: "It is not the committing of one's thought in assent to any proposition, but the trusting of one's being, there to be rested, kept, guided, molded, governed and possessed forever." Augustine said that we are made for God, and our souls are restless until they rest in Him.

Gladly and freely we surrender ourselves here and now, for all eternity, unto Thee, our Lord and Saviour. Amen.

One thing at a time!

> And Ezra the priest brought the law before the congregation both of men and women . . . and the ears of all the people were attentive unto the book of the law. (Nehemiah 8:2, 3)

A revival of true religion came about under the leadership of Ezra, through the reading of the Scriptures and the fact that the "ears of all the people were attentive to the book of the law." Luke remarks on one occasion concerning Jesus that "all the people were very attentive to hear Him." One of our most important powers is that of selecting the things to which we will give attention. In our consciousness, one thing is always in focus at the center while other things around are more or less blurred. Our mental and spiritual development depend on things to which we pay attention.

❧ We would lift up our minds and hearts to Thee, O God, and fix our thoughts more and more on the things that are eternal. Amen.

But don't rest yourself to death.

> But Jesus answered them, My Father worketh hitherto, and I work. (John 5:17)

Of the rare person who is so intemperate with his strength that he wears himself out before his time, we say, "He worked himself to death." But of how many others might we say, "He rested himself to death"? We slouch in our chairs, injuring our bodies by improper posture. If we must go a city block, we drive the car rather than get needed exercise by walking. We lounge in a movie when we might stir our minds with a serious book or a stimulating conversation. Servants keep our yards when we might find joy in digging in the good earth. And the success for which we long is not to have to work.

❧ O Thou busy God, save us from the subtle love for death, which makes us want to be idle. Amen.

It's more trouble not to think for yourself.

> My mouth shall speak of wisdom; and the meditation of my heart shall be of understanding. (Psalms 49:3)

Mental indigestion threatens or afflicts most of us. The printed page, radio, movies, and public speakers combine to fill our minds with a mass of undigested ideas. It is easier to swallow a ready-made opinion, or a lot of facts, than to think out our own conclusions. Jesus was a reader. His mind was filled with the great scriptures of His people. But what He read was processed through the mill of His own soul. "The meditation of my heart," wrote the ancient Psalmist, "shall be of understanding."

❧ Thou knowest, Father, how our age conspires against contemplation. May Thy spirit lead us into the wisdom that grows from meditation. Amen.

The man who calmly worked while the bombs fell:

> Thou wilt keep him in perfect peace, whose mind is stayed on thee: because he trusteth in thee. (Isaiah 26:3)

American troops, when they entered an Italian city that had been badly bombed, found the philosopher Santayana calmly working on a book, so Dr. Norman Vincent Peale tells us. A soldier said to him, "How can you quietly work on a book in the midst of this terrible bombardment?" Santayana smiled and said, "I am a philosopher, and philosophy is a long study. I have trained my mind to dwell on eternal matters." Dr. Peale adds: "Bombardment of nerves need not overwhelm you if you practice over a long period of time the keeping of the mind on the eternal."

Rock of Ages, who art not shaken by man's puny explosives, teach us to find refuge in Thee, where there is perfect peace. Amen.

Aim your rifle.

> . . . this one thing I do, forgetting those things which are behind, and reaching forth unto those things which are before. (Philippians 3:13)

Our age is neurotic because we are drawn in so many directions. Money, romance, leisure, power, popularity, pleasant sensations—we want all of them, and we go galloping off in all directions in pursuit of them. We end up catching none of them. Like a rifle, life is ineffective unless it is aimed. Paul could say, "This one thing I do," because he had found one thing worth giving everything for. To make a Christian commitment is to say, "My whole life shall be focused on one thing: to do the will of Christ."

Forgive us, Lord, that we have had so many gods. Give us the peace that comes with complete dedication to Thy will. Amen.

Seek both society and solitude.

> But thou, when thou prayest, enter into thy closet, and when thou hast shut thy door, pray to thy Father which is in secret . . . (Matthew 6:6)

If Jesus be our example, we shall seek both society and solitude. He loved people, and was with them on all kinds of occasions, enjoying their fellowship and entering sympathetically into their lives. He also loved solitude, frequently refreshing his spirit in healing, quiet, unhurried communion with His Father, on the mountain or by the sea.

Bless us, O God, with the strength that comes with quietness, but make us to love the companionship of people and find our joy in helping them. For Jesus' sake. Amen.

DIFFICULTY IN MAKING FRIENDS AND GETTING ALONG WITH PEOPLE

Real friends do not come cheaply.

> Henceforth I call you not servants; for the servant knoweth not what his lord doeth: but I have called you friends; for all things that I have heard of my Father I have made known unto you. (John 15:15)

We use the word "friend" very lightly. Under the expansive influence of alcohol, a man we never saw before today calls us "old pal." To casual acquaintances we write, "Dear Friend." Yet some of us go through life without making a real friend. Jesus did not call His disciples friends when He first met them, or even when they left their homes to follow Him. He called them friends when they could be told His purposes, His readiness to die for them, and when He could be confident that they would come to share His deeper life. A true friendship with one like ourselves is a beautiful benediction, but life's greatest achievement is to be a friend of Jesus.

Father, give us the qualities of spirit of which friends are made, and lead us into friendship with our Lord. Amen.

What are you willing to give to get a friend?

> . . . he died for all, that they which live should not henceforth live unto themselves, but unto him which died for them, and rose again. (II Corinthians 5:15)

In a sermon in *The Christian Century Pulpit,* Dr. Cleland McAfee told this story: "In New York City a few years ago, a man became known in some circles for his zeal in being helpful in as many ways as possible. He had a strange knack of being on hand when need arose in the personal lives of others. When he could help he did so; when he needed more help he knew how to ask it of others. He was asked one day how he came to be so active in helping other people. He replied, 'A man once died for me.' It came out that in an emergency when his life was in danger a man had thrown himself into the breach and saved him from death, though in doing so the other man lost his life. He had always felt that he owed double duty to the world for that."

O Thou who has died for us, we offer our lives to be lived for others in Thy name. Amen.

Take the initiative, and be surprised.

> But Joshua . . . shall go in thither: encourage him: for he
> shall cause Israel to inherit it. (Deuteronomy 1:38)

Moses was told to encourage Joshua, a suggestion we all frequently need to be given. John T. Faris tells of an editor who
noticed a very fine achievement of a friend and planned to
write him a letter of congratulation. After a day or two he
said to himself, "He will get hundreds of notes about it, so I
shall not bother him with mine." Later he met the friend and
told him why he had failed to send his letter of commenda-
tion. "How many do you think I received?" asked the friend.
The editor guessed many scores. But the real answer was:
"Not one!"

🍃 *For all who have encouraged us along life's way we are
grateful, Lord. Forgive us for neglecting to encourage others.
Amen.*

Three steps to a brand-new friendship:

> And when Jesus came to the place, he looked up, and saw
> him, and said unto him, Zacchaeus, make haste, and come
> down; for to day I must abide at thy house. (Luke 19:5)

David Russell of South Africa, ex-chaplain of the Black
Watch, tells of the threefold appeal of Christ to Zacchaeus.
Christ looked up into the tree and said, "Zacchaeus." Said
Zacchaeus to himself, "He knows me." Christ said, "Make
haste and come down." "Ah, He wants me," thought Zac-
chaeus. "This day I must abide at thy house." "Joy of joys,
He needs me!" thought Zacchaeus.

🍃 *We rejoice in the thought, O Christ, that we are known
to Thee and needed in Thy world. We invite Thee into our
homes and hearts. Amen.*

The one language all mankind can understand.

> She openeth her mouth with wisdom; and in her tongue is
> the law of kindness. (Proverbs 31:26)

Dr. Zamenhof, a Russian, who adopted the pseudonym Dr.
Esperanto, published a pamphlet in 1887 presenting an artificial language, which he had devised, designed to be universal. The vocabulary was based as far as possible upon
words common to the chief European languages. In 1907, in

France, another attempt at a universal language, called **Ido**, was made public. Later, a combination of the two was promulgated. No artificial attempt has been successful, though today the use of English is widespread. However, kindness is a universal language and understood by everyone.

May the kind heart of Jesus, beating in the breasts of His followers, be the magnet that will draw the world together in understanding and love. This is our prayer, Father, in His dear name. Amen.

And their upkeep is costly, too.

A friend loveth at all times, and a brother is born for adversity. (Proverbs 17:17)

No one is poor who is rich in friends. He has treasure that can neither be bought nor sold. Washington observed that friendship is a plant of slow growth and that it has to undergo and withstand the shocks of adversity before it is entitled to be called such. The price of having friends is to be a friend: "A man that hath friends must shew himself friendly." We must think about our friends, enjoy their fellowship, and let them know we love them. As Samuel Johnson said: "A man, sir, should keep his friendships in repair."

We thank Thee, O divine friend, for the friends we have made through the years. Bless them in all their interests, and make us friendly toward all mankind. Amen.

Do you impress potential friends as a sobersides?

Then was our mouth filled with laughter, and our tongue with singing: then said they among the heathen, The Lord hath done great things for them. (Psalms 126:2)

A sense of humor is one of God's best gifts. He who can laugh is welcome in any group, particularly if he can laugh at himself and if his humor carries no sting of unkindness. The ability to see the humorous side of life releases tension. Lincoln said: "With the fearful strain that is on me night and day, if I did not laugh I should die." Life is more pleasant to us and we make it better for others by enjoying fun.

We thank Thee, kind Father, for the gift of laughter. Teach us to take life seriously, without becoming gloomy. Amen.

What about your enemies?

> But I say unto you, Love your enemies . . . (Matthew 5:44)

In a sermon, Dr. Norman Vincent Peale told of the advice given by a beloved veteran politician to a young man concerned about how to fight his personal enemies: "There is only one thing to do with an enemy, only one, and that is to make a friend of him." "How can you turn any enemy into a friend?" asked the young man. "I have a little trick about that, son, that works like a charm," was the reply. "It will turn the trick if anything will. Here it is: Love your enemies, bless them that curse you, do good to them that hate you, and pray for them which despitefully use you."

❧ *God of love, we pray Thy blessing upon all who for any reason dislike us or have seemed unfriendly to us. Help us to love them and convince them that we do. Amen.*

What impression did you leave behind you today?

> A merry heart maketh a cheerful countenance: but by sorrow of the heart the spirit is broken. (Proverbs 15:13)

Curtis Courier relays this story: Bishop Manning was riding on a subway train one day when a noisy passenger, who appeared tired and exceedingly disgruntled, insulted several passengers who got in his way. When the man rose to leave, Bishop Manning remarked. "My friend, you left something here." The troublesome passenger turned, looked at his seat, then demanded, "What did I leave?" "A very bad impression," the bishop replied. The man frowned, then broke into a sheepish grin. He had the grace to answer, "I'm sorry."

❧ *We offer the prayer of the little girl: "Dear God, please make the bad people good, and the good people nice." Amen.*

Impregnable is the man who has a friend.

> He that loveth not knoweth not God; for God is love. (I John 4:8)

Impulsive John, one of the "sons of thunder" who wanted to call down fire from heaven on an inhospitable Samaritan village, was changed completely through his association with Jesus. He was profoundly impressed by the discovery that the Master loved him, and came to refer to himself as the "disciple whom Jesus loved." In that love he found God and came to feel that God is essentially love. The Father reveals Himself to us as love, and imparts to us a love for others. A Christian is conscious of being loved by God, and so loves others for His sake.

🙚 *O Thou who art love, give us a fuller assurance of Thy great love for us, and a greater measure of love for all Thy children. Amen.*

What it takes to be a friend!

> For where your treasure is, there will your heart be also. (Matthew 6:21)

A cowboy explained his idea of Christian living: "Now I'm working for Jim here. If I'd sit around, telling what a good fellow Jim is, and singing songs for him, and getting up in the night to serenade him, I'd be doing just what a lot of Christians do; but I wouldn't suit Jim, and I'd get fired mighty quick. But when I buckle on my chaps and hustle among the hills, and see that Jim's herd is all right and not suffering for lack of water and feed, or getting off range and branded by cattle thieves, then I'm proving my love and serving Jim as he wants to be served."

🙚 *Our hearts move us to praise Thee, blessed Lord, but needs around us cry out for us to serve Thee. May we neglect neither. For Jesus' sake. Amen.*

Thistles on the other side of the fence.

> . . . Know ye not that a little leaven leaveneth the whole lump? (I Corinthians 5:6)

A farmer was walking through his field with a visitor, according to a story told by Stewart Nye Hutchison. Suddenly the farmer jumped over the wall and pulled up a bunch of thistles. "Is this your land also?" asked the stranger. "No," replied the farmer, "it belongs to my neighbor. But that thistle is flowering, and soon the seed will be bown all over both fields." Thistles, disease germs, social and moral ills have a way of crossing land, race lines, and national boundaries. No man is completely safe from any danger until all are safe.

🙚 *O Father of us all, make us as diligent in defending our neighbor as ourselves from every danger. Amen.*

Friendship must be positive.

> Therefore all things whatsoever ye would that men should do to you, do ye even so to them . . . (Matthew 7:12)

Many great religions teach the Golden Rule in negative form. The Jewish Talmud says: "What is hateful to you, do not to your fellow man." The Brahmin Mahabharata says: "Do naught unto others which would cause you pain if done to you." The Buddhist Udana-Varga says: "Hurt not others in ways that you yourself would find hurtful." But followers of Jesus are taught not only to avoid harming others; they must render every service they would like to receive.

Master, may we by Thy guidance today learn a little more of what it means to live to serve the wants and needs of others. Amen.

Here is the "law of life":

> Be not deceived . . . for whatsoever a man soweth, that shall he also reap. (Galatians 6:7)

A little boy who lived in the mountains was punished severely by his mother. In a tantrum of temper he ran away screaming "I hate you; I hate you." As he paused at the edge of a ravine, the echo came back, "I hate you." Frightened, he ran back to his mother to tell of the bad man who hated him. The wise mother brought him back to the spot and told him to cry out, "I love you." The echo came back clearly, sweetly, "I love you." "That, my son," said the mother, "is the law of life. What we give, we get!"

Forgive us, Lord of the harvest, for complaining when bad seed sown has brought a faulty yield. Help us to sow spiritual seed that we may reap eternal life. Amen.

Swap places with the man next door.

> Then I came to them of the captivity . . . and I sat where they sat, and remained there astonished among them seven days. (Ezekiel 3:15)

In preparation for his ministry to the captivity, Ezekiel was sent to learn their condition. He says: "I sat where they sat." It was a revealing experience, and he says he "remained there astonished." Edwin Dahlberg says: "To better understand one another we should all swap places for a while with each

other. Every doctor should have an operation. Every police-
man and minister should spend a number of months in jail
and every industrialist became a labor union member."

❧ *Blessed Lord, who understandest us by having sat where
we sit, help us as best we can to enter sympathetically into the
lives of our fellow men. Amen.*

Three hints, if you would make a friend:

> Let every one of us please his neighbor for his good to edifi-
> cation. (Romans 15:2)

The answers to three questions should guide me in my efforts to help another. First: What does he want? "Let every
one of us please his neighbor." Second: What does he need,
"for his good"? (It is not my duty to please my neighbor with
that which will harm him.) The third question: What will
make him and all concerned finer persons—"to edification"?
Paul adds in his admonition.

❧ *Teach us, Father of us all, how to help our neighbors to
get the things they want which are good for them, and to do
it in such a way that we shall be better Christians. Amen.*

A lesson in art that can change your life:

> Thou shalt not bear false witness against thy neighbour.
> (Exodus 20:16)

The opposite of bearing false witness against a neighbor is to
speak the truth in love for him. An artist painted a portrait of
his dearest friend. When it was finished and the friend saw it,
he protested: "You have painted my portrait entirely too fine
for it to be a true likeness." "Oh, no," the artist replied, "the
features are correct. I have only painted lovingly."

❧ *God of love, give us grace to be sincere and a love for
our fellow men that will keep us from using falsehood against
them. Amen.*

You, too, may build a city of peace.

> . . . Thou shalt love thy neighbour as thyself. (Matthew
> 22:39)

An ancient legend, lovely enough to be true, tells of two

brothers who lived on adjoining farms. One had a large family, while the other had no children. Both farms produced abundant harvests. One brother said, "My brother has no family; all the joy he has is in his possessions. I will slip some of my grain into his field." The other said, "My brother has a large family. I will slip some of my grain into his field." And so they did each night, and each wondered why his harvest was not diminished, until they met one night and knew the secret. And there, the legend goes, they built the city of peace, Jerusalem.

Father of all our brothers, we think too much of how others may help us. Teach us to seek continually to help others, and so build the new Jerusalem on earth. Amen.

Give away your cake and have it, too.

And whosoever shall give to drink unto one of these little ones . . . verily I say unto you, he shall in no wise lose his reward. (Matthew 10:42)

A lovely lady tells how her mother sent her down the street at the age of ten with a bunch of sweet peas for an elderly neighbor. When she returned, her mother said, "Now smell your hand." Sniffing inquisitively, she discovered that her hand smelled like sweet peas. "Flowers always leave some of their fragrance in the hand of the giver," the mother told her. "It's that way in life, too. Every kind deed or work bestowed on someone else leaves us a sweeter person."

We thank Thee, kind Father, for the privilege of knowing people whose lives are fragrant with kindness. Help us to be like them. Amen.

But you cannot give more than what you are.

And Jesus, immediately knowing in himself that virtue had gone out of him, turned him about in the press, and said, Who touched my clothes? (Mark 5:30)

The woman who timidly touched Jesus' garment was blessed, not by what He did, but by what He was. Heaven's powers flowed through Him to those whose lives He touched. And He felt His spiritual resources expended as He blessed. If we, too, would bless others, we must keep our souls replenished by prayer. Oliver Wendell Holmes warned us: "Just so surely as you keep drawing out your soul's currency without making new deposits, the next thing will be: No Funds. Soul deposits and checks must more than just balance if we are to be spiritually dynamic."

God of all healing virtue, we desire that the touch of our lives shall bless. We wait now in Thy presence that Thou mayest fill us with Thy healing spirit. Amen.

What do you look for in people?

And as Jesus passed by, he saw a man which was blind from his birth. (John 9:1)

No two pairs of eyes ever see the same thing. The neighbors of the blind man whom Jesus healed saw only his poverty and ignoble vocation. They said: "Is not this he that sat and begged?" The disciples saw his condition as an evidence of God's displeasure. They asked: "Who did sin, this man or his parents?" What of the Master? "And as Jesus passed by, he saw a man . . . "! Christ's eyes see beyond beggar's rags, whining solicitations, and blind eyes, and are focused on the man and his needs. Do we see people as He does?

O Thou who lookest on men's hearts, help us as we walk the streets to see people as persons, made in Thy image. We pray in Jesus' name. Amen.

An answer to "Am I my brother's keeper?"

And the Lord said unto Cain, Where is Abel thy brother? And he said, I know not: Am I my brother's keeper? (Genesis 4:9)

Walter H. Judd has said: "The first moral isolationist in history was Cain. He said, 'Am I my brother's keeper?' and all of history shouts back: 'Yes, you are. You ought to be his keeper because you are his brother, but if you ignore all humanitarian reasons and consider only your own welfare, you must be his keeper in order to protect yourself. If you do not keep his legitimate interests secure, you cannot keep your own. If you do not treat him decently, ultimately he or his maladies will rise up and destroy you.' "

We pray, O loving Father, that the brotherhood of man become an experienced reality, and not just a beautiful dream. We ask it for Jesus' sake. Amen.

Be wise in your choice.

> Nevertheless the centurion believed the master and the owner of the ship, more than those things which were spoken by Paul. (The Acts 27:11)

In politics one must be wise in one's choice of advisers, to be successful. Many a promising career has been blighted by well-meaning but unwise friends. The first mark of the blessed man described in Psalm 1 was that he walked not in the counsel of the ungodly. Irreverent men are not to be trusted as life counselors. The shipwreck suffered by Paul and his fellow travelers would have been avoided if the centurion had not listened to the wrong advice. He trusted the merchant rather than the missionary.

We thank Thee, Father, for the wise and good counselors who have helped us to discover and follow right paths. Amen.

How to be a good neighbor.

> But a certain Samaritan, as he journeyed, came where he was: and when he saw him, he had compassion on him. (Luke 10:33)

The Good Samaritan was practical in his neighborliness. He used the homely remedies at hand for first aid and the donkey for transportation. He carried the injured man to an inn where there were facilities for his care. He nursed him for one night and then left him to the care of the innkeeper. He did not leave a fortune, but estimated what was needed. In the promise to pay the balance was the hint of an audit. True neighborliness seeks practical means of doing needed service.

Dear God and Father of us all, we thank Thee for those who have been neighbors to us along life's way. Enable us to keep their spirit alive in the world, in Jesus' name. Amen.

Show people your sunny side.

> Ye are the light of the world. A city that is set on an hill cannot be hid. (Matthew 5:14)

A small child was dining with her aunt and uncle. During the meal, she noticed that everyone was absorbed in matters other than herself. Hoping for a little attention, the child asked sociably, "Would anyone like to be smiled at?" Indeed, the world is full of people who need someone to smile at them.

A harassed mother of four small children says her daily prayer is, "God, keep me sane and sunny." It is a Christian prayer.

Divine Father, we believe that somehow heaven will be lighted brighter by the presence of sunny saints. May our presence make this world less dark. Amen.

And here's a test we all should take:

> He that loveth his brother abideth in the light . . . (I John 2:10)

It is impossible to look into a great boiler and see how much water it contains. But running up beside it there is a tiny glass tube, which serves as a gauge. As the water stands in the little tube, so it stands in the great boiler. When the tube is half full, the boiler is half full; when the tube is empty, the boiler is empty. Do you ask, "How do I know I love God?" Look at the gauge. Your love for your brother is the measure of your love for God.

O Thou who art love, teach us to express our love for Thee in deeds of service to Thy children. Amen.

LONELINESS

There's no more poignant unhappiness!

> Wherefore putting away lying, speak every man truth with his neighbour: for we are members one of another. (Ephesians 4:25)

There is no private sorrow or joy, no private defeat or victory, no sin or virtue that belongs to one person alone. All that happens to me concerns those who love me or are dependent upon me or whose lives are in any way linked with mine. I am glad it is so. Earth has no more poignant unhappiness than utter loneliness. Everyone needs a sense of belonging to a group, and human society needs the sense of community. Christ teaches us to make common cause with our fellows. He took on Himself the burden of humanity and commands us to follow.

Dear Father of our vast human family, teach us to weep with those who weep, rejoice with those who rejoice, and share the burdens of the heavy-laden. Amen.

Do people think you are "different"?

> Behold, I will put a fleece of wool in the floor; and if the dew be on the fleece only, and it be dry upon all the earth beside, then shall I know that thou wilt save Israel by mine hand, as thou hast said. (Judges 6:37)

Gideon asked for a sign that he might know that God was dealing with him. A fleece spread on the threshing floor was to be wet with dew, while the floor remained dry. The next night he asked that the fleece be dry and the floor wet. God's power was to be evident in making the fleece different from its environment, and in a way not explainable by natural causes. God's power can make any human life different from its environment, and the world will believe in the divine nature of Christianity only when Christians are different.

We cannot transform ourselves, O God, but as Gideon spread his fleece on the plain of Jezreel, we now spread our spirits before Thee to be filled with the heavenly dew of Thy grace. Amen.

There are different kinds of watching.

> Yea, the darkness hideth not from thee; but the night shineth as the day: the darkness and the light are both alike to thee. (Psalms 139:12)

A small boy, relates William Norton, was told that the eye of God is always watching us. He thought a minute, then said: "I'd like to know what kind of watching it is. Tim Brown watches me in school, so he can tell the teacher if I whisper and get me bad marks. But my father watches me when I'm on the beach, so I won't be in too deep. I like that kind of watching." The Psalmist despairs of escaping God, even by fleeing to the uttermost parts of the sea, but he is glad. "Even there shall Thy hand lead me, and Thy right hand shall hold me."

O Thou ever-present God, teach us the folly of fleeing from Thee, and make us to rejoice in Thine unfailing watchfulness over us. Amen.

Where can you go and not find God?

> Whither shall I go from thy Spirit? or whither shall I flee from thy presence? (Psalms 139:7)

A boy of nine was being questioned about religion by an older lad in a somewhat cynical vein, and he acquitted himself with credit. Finally the older one challenged: "I'll give you a dime if you will tell me where God is!" The prompt reply came: "I'll give you two dimes if you will tell me where He is not!"

We open our hearts to Thee, who art present here and now, gladly confident that wherever we may go Thy hand shall lead us, and Thy right hand hold us. Amen.

He never ignored an outstretched hand.

> . . . him that cometh to me I will in no wise cast out. (John 6:37)

No one who ever sought Jesus was turned away. The children brought by their parents for a blessing seemed to the disciples too small for attention, but the arms of the Master were open to them. The woman in grief for her daughter was disturbing, but He received and blessed her. The Greeks came hesitantly, doubting the possibility of actually seeing Jesus, but He was thrilled at the sight of them. Whether sick, blind, maimed, devil-possessed, or conscience-torn, all who sought Him found Him. Some turned away from Jesus, but He turned away from no one.

🙰 *O Thou always accessible Christ, receive us, with all our unlovely traits, and give us the blessings we need. Amen.*

Why be lonely when you have a friend?

> A merry heart doeth good like a medicine: but a broken spirit drieth the bones. (Proverbs 17:22)

It would seem to be the natural thing for a Christian to be happy. People in love should be happy, and a Christian is a person in love with God and people. He has the remedy for most of the causes of sadness. He need not be lonely, for he has a friend with him always. He need not be afraid, for his future is in the hands of his heavenly Father. He need not suffer remorse, for his sins are forgiven and removed as far as the east is from the west. He need not feel useless, for he is engaged in the greatest enterprise in the world.

🙰 *Blessed God, forgive us for ever having so lost sight of our privileges as to be sad. Teach us to sing and make melody in our hearts to the Lord. Amen.*

Here is the worst of all heresies:

> For we have not an high priest which cannot be touched with the feeling of our infirmities; but was in all points tempted like as we are, yet without sin. (Hebrews 4:15)

As he knelt one day in church, a character depicted by Sheila Kaye-Smith suddenly saw, with all the force of a personal revelation, a great subduing truth. "There was not one pang of his lonely, wandering life, no throb or ache or groan of his up to that moment when the light of his eyes and the desire of his heart was taken from him at a stroke, that had not been shared by God." The worst of all heresies is the thought that God has forgotten us. He can never forget us for a moment, else He would not be God.

🙰 *Lord of our lives, we face the future unafraid, knowing that our way is not hidden from Thee. May we never lose that certainty. Amen.*

So much to keep a man in touch with life!

> Who hath measured the waters in the hollow of his hand, and meted out heaven with the span, and comprehended the dust of the earth in a measure, and weighed the mountains in scales, and the hills in a balance? (Isaiah 40:12)

Sam Jones used to say: "The mountains are God's thoughts piled up. The ocean is God's thoughts spread out. The flowers are God's thoughts in bloom. The dewdrops are God's thoughts in pearls." Dwight L. Moody said that, after he was converted, everything in the world seemed more beautiful to him, because it had been made by his heavenly father. One does not really see the world unless one sees God's handiwork everywhere.

We thank Thee, O Thou Creator of all things, for the beauty and order, the wisdom and design in Thy marvelous works. Teach us to discover Thy fingerprints on them all. Amen.

You are not forgotten.

> Are not two sparrows sold for a farthing? and one of them shall not fall on the ground without your Father. But the very hairs of your head are all numbered. (Matthew 10:29, 30)

The scientists speak of the indestructibility of matter. The poet pictures the world's miser, hoarding with infinite care the rose leaves, the stars, the flowers, each blade of grass, and even the raindrops. Jesus encourages all who feel that they are forgotten, by reminding them that God never loses sight of even the tiniest bird or a hair on the head of one of His children. Nothing of value is ever lost or forgotten.

Dear watchful Father, we thank Thee for the assurance of Thy care for the little things. May we be like Thee in that no person shall seem insignificant to us. Amen.

Someone is looking for you.

> Behold the fowls of the air: for they sow not, neither do they reap, nor gather into barns; yet your heavenly Father feedeth them . . . (Matthew 6:26)

In the story told by Jesus of the straying sheep, it was not the sheep that found the shepherd, but the shepherd who found the sheep. He did not say, "I am come that the lost may be able to find me," but, "The Son of Man is come to seek and to save that which was lost." The Laodiceans were not told to knock on heaven's door, but to listen and open because heaven was knocking on their door. Most of us feel that we are Christians, not because we were so zealous in seeking God, but because He was so patient in seeking us.

O Thou good Shepherd, we thank Thee for not waiting for us to return, but that Thou didst seek us. Give us a passion to join Thee in the quest for every lost sheep of Thine. Amen.

Perhaps you found a friend today, and didn't know it.

And it came to pass, that, while they communed together and reasoned, Jesus himself drew near, and went with them. (Luke 24:15)

Our Lord sometimes travels incognito. To weeping Mary Magdalene beside the tomb He spoke comfortingly, though at first she knew Him not. On the road to Emmaus He appeared to the two and opened to them the Scriptures, but their eyes were holden that they should not recognize Him. To comfort, to guide, to reprove us, how often does Jesus walk by our side unrecognized?

O Thou risen, living Lord, make us conscious of Thy constant presence; open our minds to Thine instruction; and comfort our drooping spirits. Amen.

A leader is a lonely man.

But ye denied the Holy One and the Just . . . And killed the Prince of life, whom God hath raised from the dead; whereof we are witnesses. (The Acts 3:14, 15)

Mrs. Montgomery translates Peter's words on Solomon's porch: "The pioneer of life you put to death." "Guide of life," Weymouth puts it. The world is indebted for its progress to intrepid individuals who had the initiative and daring to strike out into undiscovered realms and blaze new trails. But pioneers are seldom popular. The farther they are in advance of their time the worse they are treated. Jesus, the pioneer of life, was crucified. And those who follow Him today are still a long way from the crowd.

Be Thou our guide, O Christ, and lead us in the narrow way that leads to life. Amen.

Great souls never follow the crowd.

> Because strait is the gate, and narrow is the way, which leadeth unto life, and few there be that find it. (Matthew 7:14)

He who would follow Jesus must be prepared to be with the minority. The Master did not apologize for that. We are told to enter the narrow way—not in spite of its narrowness, but because it is narrow, and there are few who can walk it. Great souls never follow the crowd. On any matter that requires fine moral judgment, the majority is never right. Jesus wants no followers on false pretenses. He urges us to sit down and count the cost. Then, if we are ready for it, we are to take up a cross and walk His way. There are few on the road, but what a choice company!

O God, who dost always challenge us to do our best, we gladly take the narrow road, asking only that Thou wilt lead us. Amen.

FRUSTRATIONS OF YOUTH

A young man's next victory!

> But I keep under my body, and bring it into subjection . . .
> (I Corinthians 9:27)

Bishop Hughes quotes Sir Edwin Arnold as having said, in an address to the students of our oldest university, on a visit to America: "Gentlemen of Harvard, in 1776 and 1812 you conquered your fathers. In the years from 1861 to 1865 you conquered your brothers. Will you permit an Englishman to say that your next victory must be over yourselves?" The hardest and most important victory that any man attains is over himself. Slavery to sin, another expression for being defeated by self, is the only slavery that kills.

Give us victory, O God of battles, over our most deadly enemy, who dwells within our breasts. Amen.

Did you ever test your building materials?

> Is not this the carpenter . . . ? and are not his sisters here with us? And they were offended at him. (Mark 6:3)

Jesus was a carpenter, inheriting the trade from Joseph, and all manual labor is dignified by that fact. He frequently used metaphors from His craft, calling Himself "the door," and speaking of life as laying a foundation and building a house. He is still the great builder and offers His services to everyone who is building a life. No shoddy material, no poor workmanship go into His construction. Why will anyone try to build without employing the carpenter from Nazareth?

O Thou workman of Galilee, we are serious about our task of building a life. Be Thou the architect and builder, we pray. Amen.

Have you found anything to live for?

> And he cast down the pieces of silver in the temple, and departed, and went and hanged himself. (Matthew 27:5)

Judas took his own life, not only because he felt that he was unfit to live, but even more because he had nothing for which to live. Money as a god was disappointing. He could not give allegiance to the cynical priests. And he had betrayed the Christ. Because there was a vacuum at the center of his being, where there ought to have been a supreme loyalty, life became unbearable. By contrast, Paul, who could say, "To me to live is Christ," could cry while in prison on trial for his life: "Rejoice in the Lord alway, and again I say, Rejoice."

✎ *O Thou captain of our souls, we thank Thee that in Thy kingdom on earth we have a cause worthy of our best. Help us to be loyal soldiers of our Christ. Amen.*

For the young person who has begun to doubt:

> But I know you, that ye have not the love of God in you. (John 5:42)

"Now we believe," the citizens of Sychar told the woman water carrier, "not because of thy saying; for we have heard Him ourselves, and know that this is indeed the Christ, the Saviour of the world." They had progressed from accepting another's testimony to first-hand experience. Wordsworth speaks of "one in whom persuasion and belief had ripened into faith, and faith became a passionate institution." Children usually believe what they are told about God; adults rely more on personal experience and insights. Frequently the youth who is passing from childhood belief to mature faith encounters a painful crisis. His doubts are hopeful signs of sincerity and growth, and his case is better than that of the adult who has not progressed from second-hand to first-hand experience of God.

✎ *Dear Lord, who didst deal gently with the doubts of honest Thomas, lead us through experience to an unshakable faith. Amen.*

The unlucky boy who got what he wanted.

> Ye ask, and receive not, because ye ask amiss, that ye may consume it upon your lusts. (James 4:3)

A woman was traveling with her child and a maid when a wasp flew into the carriage and the child cried for it. At last the woman said to the maid, "What is that child crying for? Let him have it!" A few minutes later the woman, startled by an awful scream from the child, exclaimed in alarm, "What's the matter?" The maid calmly replied, "He got it." We, too, sometimes cry for things that would sting us, but God is not as heartless as that maid. The war cry reminds us: "Some of our worst troubles have come from getting what we wanted. So don't complain if God doesn't answer some of your prayers."

Wise and loving Father, we thank Thee for the things Thou hast given in answer to our prayers. And we are not less grateful for Thy withholding the things that would have hurt us. Amen.

One kind of running that's not cowardly.

> And when the woman saw that the tree was good for food, and that it was pleasant to the eyes, and a tree to be desired to make one wise, she took of the fruit thereof, and did eat, and gave also unto her husband with her; and he did eat. (Genesis 3:6)

In the story of the subtle serpent, Eve's doom was sealed when she entered into friendly conversation with the tempter. Paul cautioned young Timothy to run away from temptation. A young person is already defeated when he begins to think of temptation as something interesting to be experimented with, rather than something dangerous to be avoided. Odysseus, in the ancient legend, escaped the sirens' lure by filling his sailors' ears with wax and lashing himself to the mast.

Our Father who art in heaven, lead us not into temptation, but deliver us from evil. Amen.

Do you have ambitions that look too far?

> . . . Except ye be converted; and become as little children, ye shall not enter into the kingdom of heaven. (Matthew 18:3)

What is the invariable characteristic of childhood? It is not innocence, for children are sometimes rather naughty. Nor is it teachability, for they can be quite perverse. Is it not rather growth? No child is merely six years old; he is "six, going on seven." Always he is reaching forward and upward. So is the child of God in his spiritual infancy, and only eternity will reveal his full mature stature.

Father of our spirits, we are ashamed of our littleness, but glory in the assurance of what we by Thy grace are to become. Amen.

Something practical about pulling up habits.

> Train up a child in the way he should go: and when he is old, he will not depart from it. (Proverbs 22:6)

On a stroll through a forest with a shiftless youth, a wise old man stopped and pointed to four plants. The first was a tiny sprout, the next a bit larger, the third a sturdy shrub, and the fourth a tree. The old man said, "Pull up the tiny plant," and the youth did it easily. The next took more effort, and the third required all his strength. But the tree defied all the youth's efforts. "Just so," said the wise old man, "with our habits. When full-grown, they cannot be uprooted." A distinguished penologist has said, "The place to stop crime is not in the electric chair, but in the high chair."

🙋 *Our prayer today, good Father, is for all parents, teachers and leaders of children, that they may mold beautifully the plastic clay entrusted to their hands. Amen.*

Slowest of all to a young person is—time.

> But when the fulness of the time was come, God sent forth his Son . . . (Galatians 4:4)

We men are fussy, fidgety, impatient. We think that if we were God, we would make things happen in a hurry. When earthquakes, tornadoes, and floods come, we feel that God is moving. Yet the great works of God are done slowly. Time is His great instrument. From all eternity He had had it in His heart to give His Son, but only when the time had fully come did Christ appear. God is patient. Tertullian said of the Pharisees and Christ: "They should have known that He was God. His patience should have proved it to them."

🙋 *O Thou unhurried, eternal God, who hast in the fulness of time brought us into the world, show us our part in the work Thou art doing among men. Amen.*

Shaky feet, when you try them alone!

> For the Father himself loveth you, because ye have loved me, and have believed that I came out from God. (John 16:27)

A father and son had been inseparable for the thirty-two years of the son's life. They were companions in recreation and partners in business, and the younger man had never made an important decision without deferring to his father's wishes. Then the father died. Crushed and a little bitter, the son felt that God had dealt unfairly in taking away his father. Years have passed and he can now see that he did not mature until he had to stand on his own feet and make his own decisions. Just so it was best for the disciples that Jesus should go away, in order that their leadership might begin to come from within themselves.

Teach us, O divine Spirit, to walk confidently in the light that Thou dost give directly to us. Amen.

Astronomers and daughters!

As free, and not using your liberty for a cloke of maliciousness, but as the servants of God. (I Peter 2:16)

James Truslow Adams has said: "Any astronomer can predict with absolute accuracy just where every star in the heavens will be at half-past eleven tonight. He can make no such predictions about his young daughter." Precisely! And unless she be very young, it is better so. It is better not to know where she will be, better to be confident that she will be doing right than to have her under lock and key, and be unable to trust her. God is interested in rearing children that He can trust with freedom.

As free beings, we choose to glorify Thee, O God, and to follow gladly Thy loving leadership. Amen.

Life seems to move so slowly, and you grow impatient!

For we are labourers together with God: ye are God's husbandry, ye are God's building. (I Corinthians 3:9)

Workmen who are builders of the City of God sometimes feel that no progress is being made, but under the guidance of the Great Architect each can add something to the structure. "One day," relates Louis E. Thayer, "I came upon a gang of men who were building a mammoth wall. I said to one of the workers, 'That's a mighty big job you have on your hands.' He laughed and replied, 'It isn't so bad. You do it one brick at a time.'"

Master, keep clear before us the dream of the city that Thou art building, and keep us faithful to our task in it. Amen.

A whole life at stake in just one seed!

> For unto every one that hath shall be given, and he shall
> have abundance: but from him that hath not shall be taken
> away even that which he hath. (Matthew 25:29)

Recently I visited a plant where various kinds of seed are
prepared for sale to farmers. I was impressed with the many
careful processes through which the tiny seeds are carried so
as to be sure that they are unmixed with other kinds of seeds,
unpolluted by diseases, and uninfested with pests. "Why," I
asked, "so much trouble for a tiny seed?" The foreman explained: "A whole year of work is at stake in the seed a
farmer plants. No matter how hard he works, if he plants poor
seed, he'll make a poor crop." So in life's harvest, Paul warns
us: "Whatsoever a man soweth, that shall he also reap."

*Make us wise, O God, in the seed that we daily plant,
and quietly content to leave the fruition to Thee. Amen.*

Only two letters, but the hardest word of all!

> . . . be it known unto thee, O king, that we will not serve
> thy gods, nor worship the golden image which thou hast set
> up. (Daniel 3:18)

Edward W. Bok reminisced: "I remember when as a boy I
asked my father once which, to his mind, was the hardest
word in the English language. Without a moment's hesitation
he answered, 'No!' 'No?' I echoed in surprise. 'Exactly,' he
answered. 'Not in spelling, as I suppose you mean. But you
will find as you go along that it is the hardest word in the
English language.' I did. And difficult to say it was at times,
as my father had predicted."

*Give us wisdom and courage, O God, always to say "No"
to every tempting evil, however winsome, and "Yes" to Thee,
however great the cost. Amen.*

Are you sure your car is going somewhere?

> I press toward the mark for the prize of the high calling of
> God in Christ Jesus. (Philippians 3:14)

Two boys boarded a train, walked back to an empty com-
partment, and sat down. A porter looked in and said, "Would
you mind moving to the next car?" "But we prefer to stay
here." The man said, "The next car is just like this one."

"But we like to be by ourselves. Why can't we stay here?"
And they settled back in their seats. "It's all right with me,"
the porter told them, "but this car ain't hitched to nothin'
and it ain't goin' nowhere." Some of us have been more interested in a comfortable place to relax than in the goal toward which we were moving.

*Thou who didst steadfastly set Thy face toward Jerusa-
lem, keep our faces set toward our highest destinies. Amen.*

Here's help for a good beginning:

> Be not deceived . . . for whatsoever a man soweth, that
> shall he also reap. (Galatians 6:7)

The preparation of the seedbed and choice of good seed are
the most important operations in farming. The common saying, "A bad beginning makes a good ending," is never true in
anything. Byron, who died at thirty-six confessing that his
life was in the "sear and yellow leaf," wrote: "The thorns I
have reaped are of the tree I planted. They have torn me, and
I bleed! I should have known what fruit would spring from
such seed." For a good day, a task well done, or a life well
spent, start right.

*For all who are laying foundations, for all who are sow-
ing seed, for all who are making important beginnings, we
pray Thy guidance, Lord, in Jesus' name. Amen.*

CONFLICTS IN MARRIAGE

Mathematically right, but all wrong!

> Doth not behave itself unseemly, seeketh not her own, is not easily provoked, thinketh no evil. (I Corinthians 13:5)

A young man who was dating several girls sat down and wrote out a list of traits: intelligence, health, domesticity, looks, sex appeal. He weighed each girl's score against the list, found the one that rated highest, and married her. They were far from happy. He had looked for the girl who had most to offer him rather than the one to whom he wanted to give everything.

God of love, who didst reveal Thyself by giving Thy Son, may we so love Thee and our brothers that we shall find happiness in giving ourselves. Amen.

Do your children provoke you?

> But God commendeth his love toward us, in that, while we were yet sinners, Christ died for us. (Romans 5:8)

Harold S. Hulbert writes: "Children need love, especially when they do not deserve it." Regardless of how any child may have come to have an unlovely disposition, the best and most effective remedy is to love him. It is not easy to love the unlovely, even in children, but that is the only way to work the miracle of regeneration. That which is true of the little child is true of us all. "But God commendeth His love toward us, in that, while we were yet sinners, Christ died for us."

Dear Jesus, we want to be like Thee, loving those who are least lovely, because they need love the most. Amen.

The most important thing a lad can do.

> But grow in grace, and in the knowledge of our Lord and Saviour Jesus Christ. To him be glory both now and for ever. Amen. (II Peter 3:18)

A little boy in kindergarten, when asked, "Who made you?" replied, "God made me about so big, and I growed the rest of the way." A young couple were watching their little son busily engaged with his erector set. "I wonder what he's making," the wife whispered. "The most important thing in the world," the father answered. "He's making a man!" The most important thing any little boy is doing is growing. And more important than the development of his body is the growth of his mind and spirit. Physical growth is completed early, but soul growth goes on throughout life.

🕊 *Great author of life, we thank Thee for the processes by which our bodies grow. Keep us youthful and growing in spirit always. Amen.*

And give some thought to the children.

> But Jesus called them unto him, and said, Suffer little children to come unto me, and forbid them not . . . (Luke 18:16)

It is said that when Kagawa was striving to reclaim outcasts in the city slums of Japan, a friend suggested that it would be better to begin with the boys and girls. Kagawa answered that he was unwilling to wait until they had grown up to see the results of his labor. A quarter of a century later he said: "I must confess that I made a serious mistake. If I had put more energy into the winning of children for Christ, I should probably have been more successful. I was too impatient to wait ten or fifteen years for them to become adults." Short-sighted indeed is the minister, the church, or the community that neglects its children!

🕊 *Give us wisdom, God of the future, to mold wisely the pliable lives of the children. Amen.*

An old way to spell "love".

> For God so loved the world, that he gave his only begotten Son, that whosoever believeth in him should not perish, but have everlasting life. (John 3:16)

A young man fell in love with a lovely girl, a rare and beautiful spirit, who was an invalid. They have been married seven years, and she is not doing well. He has spent his money, his strength, his time, and all he had for her. His one regret is that his all has not been enough. He loves her, so he has given. Love is the most expensive thing in the world. The way to spell love is G-I-V-E. The measure of God's love was His gift, and that was unmeasured. The Son was His life, His dearest treasure, His all. To love God and His poor world will cost us our all.

❦ *Father, we thank Thee for Thy love to us. May Thy Spirit, which is love, fill our hearts and direct our lives. For Jesus' sake. Amen.*

What's wrong with a ball-and-chain?

> The heart of her husband doth safely trust in her, so that he shall have no need of spoil. (Proverbs 31:11)

Carl Jung, the famous psychologist, observed that all married people wear chains. Someone asked Dr. Albert E. Wiggam for his thought on that statement. "Certainly, they do," he replied. "I've been wearing them for years and I give Dr. Jung prolonged applause. People get married because they want to wear a lot of chains . . . chains that bind them together happily in their struggles to solve the problems of life." To our dear ones here, and to Christ, we delight to be "together linked with adamantine chains."

❦ *Grateful for the strong ties of love that bind us to our dear ones and to Thee, blessed Lord, we desire not release from them, but that they may stronger grow. Amen.*

A man whose wife left him.

> Come, and let us return unto the Lord: for he hath torn, and he will heal us; he hath smitten, and he will bind us up. (Hosea 6:1)

The love story of Hosea is touching and pitiful. His beloved wife proved unfaithful, and finally left with her lovers. Then, after a long time, he found her in a slave market, paid the price of her redemption, and led her back to his home. From that tragic experience came the clear vision of Israel as the unfaithful beloved of Jehovah, and the call to prophesy. His pleas to his people have been called more sob than language, but his conception of the love of God was nearer to that of Jesus than any other Old Testament writer. The most tragic experiences sometimes bring about the deepest understanding of God.

❦ *Nearer, my God, to Thee, nearer to Thee; e'en though it be a cross that raiseth me. Amen.*

Maybe your trouble is—you!

> And the peace of God, which passeth all understanding, shall keep your hearts and minds through Christ Jesus. (Philippians 4:7)

Our happiness depends much more on what we are than where we are. A young woman who lived under discordant home conditions grew so dissatisfied that her discontent was evident in her face, her manner, and the tone of her voice. She would gladly have traveled far to get away from her disagreeable environment. Later, a friend met her and saw in her smiling face that a change had taken place. "How are things at home?" he inquired. "Just the same," she replied, "but I am different."

May Thy spirit of peace, O God, keep the portals of our hearts, that the enemies of our peace be not allowed to enter. Amen.

Thoughtfulness: the word your wife loves!

> And the second time the cock crew. And Peter called to mind the word that Jesus said unto him, Before the cock crow twice, thou shalt deny me thrice. And when he thought thereon, he wept. (Mark 14:72)

Peter wept over his denials of Christ when he stopped to think, the implication being that he had denied because he did not think. Franklin used to say that carelessness does more harm than want of knowledge. In our homes, most of us neglect to express our love, appreciation, and interest in dear ones. We could make life far more pleasant for those around us simply by being more thoughtful.

O Thou who dost never forget Thine own, teach us not only to have good will, but to be thoughtful of the feelings of others. Amen.

The kindliest relationship in the world:

> And the angel came in unto her, and said, Hail, thou that art highly favoured, the Lord is with thee: blessed art thou among women. (Luke 1:28)

Womanhood was never so honored as in the birth of our Lord. A tender and holy light seems to linger around the Virgin Mother throughout both of the gospel stories of the event. The kindness and consideration of Jesus for women, even fallen women, was in marked contrast with the customs of His day. A Hindu woman said to a missionary: "Surely your Bible was written by a woman." "Why?" he asked. "Because it says so many kind things for women. Our pundits never refer to us but in reproach."

❧ *We rejoice, dear Son of Mary, in what Thou hast done for womanhood and in what godly womanhood has done for Thee. Amen.*

Triflers need not apply.

Thou shalt not commit adultery. (Exodus 20:14)

The marriage relation is the next most sacred thing to life itself. In it one man and one woman determine to unite their two separate destinies, freely pledging their lifelong devotion. The life of the two together can be far more wonderful than can the life of two lived separately, especially when there are children. The most powerful drives of personality become glorified and creative. It is wrong to trifle with affections, as it is wrong to trifle with human life, and for the same reason: because human personality is sacred.

❧ *From the blessedness of our sweetest relations here, dear Christ, may we learn to give ourselves utterly to Thee. Amen.*

"Do as I say!" you tell your children.

Let no man despise thy youth; but be thou an example . . .
in conversation, in charity, in spirit, in faith, in purity.
(I Timothy 4:12)

An old man whose life had not been consistent with his Christian profession complained to his pastor: "I can't understand why my boys live like they do. I've told them every day of their lives that those things don't pay. I'm too old to change much, but I've tried to teach my boys right." An old Chinese proverb says: "Not the cry but the flight of the wild duck leads the flock to fly and follow." In order that his ministry might be effective, Paul advised young Timothy: "Be thou an example of the believers."

❧ *We thank Thee, Lord, for those whose lips have taught us truth, but most of all for those whose steps have led us aright. Amen.*

More than you think depends on your home.

> And the Lord said unto Noah, Come thou and all thy house into the ark; for thee have I seen righteous before me . . . (Genesis 7:1)

Noah and his wife were successful home builders. When the world was flooded with wickedness, the patriarch walked with God and kept his family devout. When the waters came, he and his little brood were safe in the ark he had built. It became his home and, although its hospitality was offered to the neighbors, only his family found refuge in it. But in building a home that was safe for his own family, Noah saved the future of the entire race. In every generation the future of mankind depends on godly homes.

Father, who hast given us the hope of a heavenly home, and a foretaste of it in our earthly homes, grant us grace and wisdom to make these homes secure. Amen.

Give your flowers today.

> Then took Mary a pound of ointment . . . and anointed the feet of Jesus . . . and the house was filled with the odour of the ointment. (John 12:3)

Nicodemus and Joseph of Arimathea did a beautiful thing in making loving provision for the body of Jesus. But Mary of Bethany did a lovelier thing when, while He yet lived, she poured out on her adored friend her sweetest and most precious possession. She did not calculate the cost nor try to save a part to sell. John tells us that "the house was filled with the odour of the ointment." The sweetest fragrance that can fill any house is the atmosphere created where love is freely expressed.

Father God, whose intimate name is love, teach us to give natural expression to our finest impulses. We ask it in Jesus' name. Amen.

Have you learned to give, in the home?

> . . . remember the words of the Lord Jesus, how he said, It is more blessed to give than to receive. (The Acts 20:35)

It is blessed to receive. The wages of our honest toil are needed for us to live. There is happiness in having our loved ones express their love to us by gifts. God's generosity crowns our lives with blessings. But it is more blessed to give. A mother giving herself in love to the care of her baby reaps richer rewards than the child does. It is better to be the compassionate host than the lucky beggar. Greater is God who giveth to all liberally than the most fortunate of creatures. Man is most happy, most noble, and most like his heavenly Father when he gives freely.

Dear gracious Father, forgive us the folly of thinking to find happiness in getting. May we learn more and more the joy of Christ-like giving. Amen.

What have the two of you to share?

Except the Lord build the house, they labour in vain that build it . . . (Psalms 127:1)

James Gray in his novel, *Shoulder the Sky*, tells of two young people whose marriage had failed. As they were parting, the two tried to analyze their difficulties. In the course of the conversation the husband said: "Our shared doubts have been the only thing we had in common. They were not enough." They never are. The only safe foundation for building a home is a shared faith in God. Families that pray together stay together, and those that worship together grow together.

On this Thy day, O God, we rededicate our homes to Thee, and seek Thy guidance in sanctifying them. Amen.

Perhaps you have a home, or just a house.

Through wisdom is an house builded; and by understanding it is established. (Proverbs 24:3)

Bruce Barton has said that many a man who pays rent all his life owns his own home, and that many a family that has saved up money for a home finds itself with nothing but a house. Edgar A. Guest wrote: "It takes a heap o' livin' in a house t' make it home." Someone observed that rather: "It takes a heap o' lovin' in a house t' make it home." It is love that makes a home, however modest the building.

Grateful for the joys of home, Father, we pray that the spirit of love and brotherhood may spread to all mankind. Amen.

Do not accept, or give, substitutes.

> Train up a child in the way he should go: and when he is old, he will not depart from it. (Proverbs 22:6)

Modern psychology has discovered anew the importance of environment during the first half-dozen years of life. Basic attitudes of trust or distrust, friendliness or retreat from social contacts, openness or secretiveness, are largely the product of those early years. A child whose parents love and trust each other, and who is sure of their love for him, feels secure, not only in childhood, but throughout life. There is not and cannot be a substitute for the Christian home.

O Thou who hast taught us to call Thee Father, we honor those who made that name sacred to us. Give guidance and grace to the homemakers of the world. Amen.

SOCIAL HANDICAPS

The easy solution solves nothing.

> And his disciples came and besought him, saying, Send her away; for she crieth after us. (Matthew 15:23)

The Canaanitish woman, crying: "Lord, have mercy on me, for my daughter is grievously vexed with a devil," disturbed the disciples. She was a human being in distress, and that made them uncomfortable. They were the more embarrassed because she was of a despised race. So they proposed a simple solution: "Send her away." How natural it is to want to get human misery and social ills out of sight! But Jesus knew that devils and suffering, faith and love, are not barred by racial lines, and His compassion could not look the other way.

Dear Father God, forgive our impulse to push unpleasant conditions out of our sight, and teach us to love and help all who need us. Amen.

Do you look at color or character?

> . . . I perceive that God is no respecter of persons. (The Acts 10:34)

Application blanks for entrance to Brandeis University have room only for educational information. No questions are asked as to ancestry, religion, mother's maiden name, etc. In this way the applicant's eligibility is decided solely on his academic qualifications. Peter declared: ". . . I perceive that God is no respecter of persons."

God of all mankind, show us how unfair and foolish are our prejudices and teach us to see Thine image in every man. Amen.

Let a Negro scientist challenge you.

> And the Lord said unto him, What is that in thine hand? And he said, A rod. (Exodus 4:2)

Following the idea suggested in these words to its great founder, Tuskegee Institute in Alabama has specialized in giving vocational training to the underprivileged Negro youth of the South, teaching them the dignity of labor and something of its limitless possibilities. George Washington Carver, who taught and experimented at Tuskegee for many years, produced hundreds of useful products from common clay, sweet potatoes, and peanuts. To the Southern Negro youth this man said, "What is that in thine hand?" and then showed them what to do with what they had.

❧ *O God our helper, teach us to see how miraculous are the common things of life, and by their use to show forth Thy glory. Amen.*

They stepped over the barriers and found peace.

> And he touched her hand, and the fever left her: and she arose, and ministered unto them. (Matthew 8:15)

There were two people who Jesus said had great faith: the centurion whose servant was sick, and the Canaanitish woman whose daughter was "grievously vexed with a devil." The two had other things in common: both were Gentiles and came to Jesus across racial barriers; each came on a mission of love, the soldier pleading for his servant who was dear to him, the woman interceding for her stricken daughter. Great faith, then, is humble, catholic, selfless.

❧ *Dear Father of all the races of men, give us faith that will dissolve pride and prejudice and selfishness. We ask it in Jesus' name. Amen.*

This is your business.

> Therefore all things whatsoever ye would that men should do to you, do ye even so to them . . . (Matthew 7:12)

Without owning a slave, Lincoln felt himself involved in the institution of slavery. He lived in a social organization of which slavery was a part. If cheap cotton goods, for instance, were available because of slave labor, every buyer of them was working slaves. Lincoln had power to do something toward their freedom. Every man is responsible for his use of power. So, when any person fights to right a social wrong, he is not meddling in that which does not concern him; he is attending to his own business.

❧ *Father and God of us all, make us to see clearly the responsibilities that are inseparable from our privileges. Amen.*

Do only white men achieve distinction?

> There is neither Jew nor Greek, there is neither bond nor free, there is neither male nor female: for ye are all one in Christ Jesus. (Galatians 3:28)

Parent-Teacher Magazine reminds us that fifty years ago, when the first edition of *Who's Who in America* was published, not one Negro's name was listed. The current edition carries the biographies of ninety-two eminent men and women of the Negro race, including statesmen, scholars, artists, and scientists. This is a tribute to their own efforts, but it is a source of gratitude to all who believe in the teachings of Jesus concerning brotherhood.

❧ *We thank Thee, Father of us all, for the progress made toward overcoming racial injustice. May we go forward in love that only Thou canst give. Amen.*

But when you know a man, he looks different.

> And Nathanael said unto him, Can there any good thing come out of Nazareth? Philip saith unto him, Come and see. (John 1:46)

A white man said: "All Negroes look alike to me." On another occasion a Negro asked: "Don't you think all Chinese look alike?" The first confessed that he had no Negro friends, and the other that he knew no Chinese people. A well-dressed man walked down the street and noticed only a group of laborers. A hod carrier saw only a car full of young society folk passing. How hard it is for us to see individual human beings across racial, national and economic lines! Will Rogers said: "I never met a man I didn't like." Perhaps the reason we don't like each other is that we have never really met.

❧ *O God, help us to break down the barriers that separate Thy children. For Jesus' sake. Amen.*

Why not blue eyes vs. brown eyes?

> And hath made of one blood all nations of men for to dwell on all the face of the earth . . . (The Acts 17:26)

To those who have been "renewed in knowledge after the image of Him that created them," there is neither Greek nor Jew, circumcised nor uncircumcised, barbarian, Scythian, bonded nor free. But, "Christ is all and in all." Superficial distinctions are simply not recognized, just as in a harmonious family where there are blondes and brunettes these are not divided against each other. The superficial difference is forgotten. Christians may have racial prejudice, but the prejudice is not Christian. The spirit of Christ is the only hope for our having "one world."

✒ *O Thou universal Christ, save all mankind from sin, and especially from the sin of unbrotherly pride. We ask it in Jesus' name. Amen.*

Let's share our loaf.

> And the Pharisees and scribes murmured, saying, This man receiveth sinners, and eateth with them. (Luke 15:2)

A woman's club in Chicago canceled an engagement with Countee Cullen, because it was their custom to have tea with their speakers, and they felt that they could not do that with the colored poet. Someone commented: "Poems are made by fools like me, but only God can come to tea." The question of eating with one's "inferiors" was raised frequently by critics of Jesus. They asked His disciples: "Why do ye eat and drink with publicans and sinners?" Of the Master they exclaimed in horror: "This man receiveth sinners, and eateth with them." So they charged Peter: "Thou wentest in to men uncircumcised, and didst eat with them." They did not criticize him for preaching Christ to Cornelius, but argued that he must not treat him like a brother by eating with him. Is there not special significance in the fact that our Lord ordained a meal to be eaten by His followers together?

✒ *Thou who dost give and bless our bread, teach us the fellowship of sharing our loaf with every brother man. Amen.*

Greatness recognizes no color line.

> . . . God gave them the like gift as he did unto us . . . (The Acts 11:17)

Dr. Benjamin Mays, in his excellent booklet, *Seeking to Be Christian in Race Relations,* quotes the anthropologist Franz Boas: "If we were to select the most intelligent, imaginative, energetic, and emotionally stable third of mankind, all races would be represented." Rabindranath Tagore of Bengal is one of the great poets of modern time. T. Z. Koo, a Chinese, and Toyohiko Kagawa, a Japanese, are among the leading

Christians of our day. Mahatma Gandhi, an Indian, was, after Jesus, the greatest exponent of nonviolence. Dr. Mays, a Negro, is a great educator. God has raised up significant people from every race.

Forgive our foolish pride of race, O God of all the earth, and teach us to look beyond the color of skin to see the divine image in every man. Amen.

A story of widened horizons.

> . . . when he departed, he took out two pence, and gave them to the host, and said unto him, Take care of him; and whatsoever thou spendest more, when I come again, I will repay thee. (Luke 10:35)

The story of the Good Samaritan pushed neighborly responsibility a little farther at every point. The needy man was not only a stranger, he was a foreigner. He was not only of a different race, he was of an unfriendly race. The Samaritan not only showed sympathy, he did something. He not only treated the wounds, he hired someone else to take care of the victim. He not only paid the bill, he assumed responsibility for whatever more might be required. Christian neighborliness consists not in doing the necessary service but in seeking the extra that we may do.

We thank Thee, Father, for occasions to be of service to others. Teach us to welcome them as opportunities. Amen.

What, after all, do "big" and "little" mean?

> And they brought young children to him, that he should touch them: and his disciples rebuked those that brought them.
> But when Jesus saw it, he was much displeased, and said unto them, Suffer the little children to come unto me, and forbid them not: for of such is the kingdom of God. (Mark 10:13, 14)

Jesus was criticized often for His failure to recognize the distinction between important people and the unimportant, between the big people and little ones, between respectable people and the despised, and even between righteous people and the unrighteous. His critics did not understand that Jesus saw so much that was precious in even the humblest that He could not despise anyone. To Him even the most unprepossessing person was made in the image of God, and so was

of infinite worth. Yet the greatness this world honors seemed
to Him a hollow mockery.

*~ O God in whose hand our little lives are lived, grant us
to see Thine image in every living soul. May we honor the
things of the spirit, and not the pride of the flesh. Amen.*

Watch out for vague generalities.

Then Peter and the other apostles answered and said, We
ought to obey God rather than men. (The Acts 5:29)

To Peter's declaration, "We ought to obey God," no one objected. When he interpreted that to mean, "We ought to
preach Jesus in Jerusalem now," the fight was on. By dealing
in generalities, men can agree on high principles. Conflicts
arise when principles are applied in actual situations. We
ought to be Christian in race relations, we agree, but to ap-
ply the principle in practical brotherhood raises conflicts. We
believe Christ ought to dictate industrial peace, but the fur
flies when we interpret His terms of peace.

*~ O Thou who art the guide of our lives, keep us firm in
our hold on the great principles of righteousness, and diligent
in applying them daily. Amen.*

Here's one to remember.

And hath made of one blood all nations of men for to dwell
on all the face of the earth . . . (The Acts 17:26)

Seeing Diogenes looking attentively at a large collection of
human bones piled one upon another, Alexander the Great
asked the philosopher what he was looking for. "I am search-
ing for the bones of your father," replied the wise man, "but
I cannot distinguish them from those of his slaves."

*~ Save us, O God, from pride in things which cannot sur-
vive the grave, and teach us the true equality of all mankind
before Thee. Amen.*

"The world is one; we cannot live apart."

For God so loved the world, that he gave his only begotten
Son, that whosoever believeth in him should not perish,
but have everlasting life. (John 3:16)

I have read that in ancient Babylon maps were made on

which Babylon covered the greater part of the planet. The rest was vague and small. How many of us today have, in our minds, at least, a Babylonian chart of the world, with our town, our state, or our nation occupying almost all the space? Jesus came because God loved the world. If our hearts are not big enough to take in the world, they are too small. If our arms are not long enough to embrace the globe, they are too short.

❧ *Forgive provincial narrowness, O Father of us all, and help us, like Thee, to love the world. We pray in the name of the world's Saviour. Amen.*

ILL HEALTH AND PHYSICAL HANDICAPS

Even a shut-in can do this much.

> I thank my God upon every remembrance of you. (Philippians 1:3)

I have a friend who is an invalid, and seems unable to do any useful work. But she does a service that is much needed. She approves! No, she doesn't approve everything, but she does give much attention to the blameworthy. She hears my sermons and she always does me good with her approval, not because of the compliments, but because of the wisdom with which she selects the things to approve. Many a young person has begun to neglect doing important things, after holding to them for a long time, simply for lack of the assurance that someone has noticed and approved.

O Thou God of praise, keep us reminded of the good we can do by commending that which is praiseworthy. Amen.

When the doctor says, "Now this will hurt—"

> Now no chastening for the present seemeth to be joyous, but grievous: nevertheless afterward it yieldeth the peaceable fruit of righteousness unto them which are exercised thereby. (Hebrews 12:11)

A skilled surgeon about to perform a delicate operation upon the ear said reassuringly, "I may hurt you, but I will not injure you." The patient could only trust in the judgment and skill of the physician who would inflict necessary pain regretfully in order to heal. How often the Great Physician gives to us the same assurance, if we would only listen!

Bless the Lord, O my soul . . . who healeth all thy diseases . . . even at the cost of pain to both. Amen.

Your scars may be your credentials.

> As many were astonied at thee . . . (Isaiah 52:14)

Adoniram Judson is said to have gone to the Burman king, after a horrible twenty-one months in Let-Ma-Yoon prison, to ask permission to go to another village to preach. The permission was denied him, though he was told he might send another. The king's reason was that his people would not believe the Christian faith when simply stated, but by seeing the crippled and scarred hands of the missionary who had suffered so much for Christ, they would be convinced. Thomas would not believe in the risen Lord until he had seen the scars. Paul offered as his credentials: "I bear in my body the marks of the Lord Jesus."

Forgive us, Lord, that we have shrunk from even the smallest inconvenience for Thy sake. Send upon us whatever suffering we can use to glorify Thee. Amen.

Three ways you may be healed:

Who forgiveth all thine iniquities; who healeth all thy diseases. (Psalms 103:3)

God heals our diseases in at least three ways. First, He uses the processes of nature. The recuperative powers of our bodies are His works, and all the discoveries of medical science are but a means of cooperating with Him. He heals through human compassion. Jesus always healed the sick, and those who share His spirit work for better health conditions and medical service. God also responds to prayer and faith. Doctors are recognizing more and more the effect of spirit on body. A reliant faith that brings spiritual peace and moral victory is a healer of diseases.

Our good Father, we trust Thee for strength for today's tasks, and pray for Thy healing power in the bodies of all who suffer, in the name of Him who was called The Healer. Amen.

The kind of beauty you can't buy.

Whose adorning let it not be that outward adorning of plaiting the hair, and of wearing of gold, or of putting on apparel;
But let it be the hidden man of the heart, in that which is not corruptible, even the ornament of a meek and quiet spirit, which is in the sight of God of great price. (I Peter 3:3, 4)

A critical preacher, speaking to a small group, was quoting the astounding statistics on the amount of money spent by American women on cosmetics, when a brother interrupted to say, "Yes, preacher, and it ain't enough!" Cosmetics may help, but no amount of money can buy beauty. Spiritual qualities are essential. Recently I saw a lovely photograph of a vase of flowers, and was told that they were lighted from behind, so that the petals shone as though aglow. A little girl, remembering the stained-glass windows in church, said, "A saint is a person that the light shines through."

However irregular our features, Father, help us to make our souls beautiful. Amen.

Do you think your obstacle is insuperable?

Yea, though I walk through the valley of the shadow of death, I will fear no evil: for thou art with me . . . (Psalms 23:4)

The Latin poet Horace said that adversity has the effect of eliciting talents which in prosperous circumstances would have lain dormant. "Live undaunted," he counseled, "and oppose gallant breasts against the strokes of adversity." Some of the greatest men and women who have lived have overcome seemingly insuperable obstacles. Glenn Cunningham became the world's greatest mile runner after burns had made it improbable that he would ever walk again. "By my God," wrote the Psalmist, "have I leaped over a wall."

We thank Thee, kind Father, for the adversity that has developed our sinews. Amen.

Your pain can be a blessing.

And he took the cup, and gave thanks, and gave it to them, saying, Drink ye all of it. (Matthew 26:27)

Jesus took the cup that was a symbol of His shed blood, and gave thanks. He was saying, "I thank God for my suffering." To love deeply, to grow strong, to know happiness, we must suffer. Pain can be a blessing. His was also the cup of duty, and Jesus was grateful for a sense of destiny: "For this cause came I into the world." It is good to feel that one's life has meaning in God's plan. His was the cup of devotion, and Jesus was saying, "I am thankful for the love I feel." Life is rich to anyone who loves enough to die for his beloved.

Dear Father, we thank Thee for life's cup of suffering and duty and love. Help us always to say, "Thy will be done." Amen.

Adversity can be your ladder to success.

> For by thee I have run through a troop; and by my God have I leaped over a wall. (Psalms 18:29)

Some of the most conspicuous examples of achievement have been men and women who made their way in spite of what must have appeared to them insuperable obstacles. Two of the greatest epic poets, Homer and Milton, were blind. Helen Keller, though blind and deaf, is credited with achievements rarely attained by anyone without handicap. To be obliged to struggle with adversity is not an unmitigated evil. To the determined soul it can be a ladder of success. The Latin poet Horace observed that adversity has the effect of eliciting talents which in prosperous circumstances would have lain dormant.

~ *O God, our strength, we do not ask for lighter burdens, but for strength to carry the load that is ours. In Jesus' name we ask it. Amen.*

Worse even than blinded eyes!

> And Jesus said, For judgment I am come into this world, that they which see not might see; and that they which see might be made blind. (John 9:39)

Helen Keller, deprived of sight and hearing by illness in infancy, soon became dumb. When Helen was six, a twenty-year-old girl, Anne Sullivan, came to teach her. Within a month the child was speaking. She was graduated from Radcliffe College *cum laude.* She mastered several languages and wrote books marked by a beautiful sensitiveness of spirit. She wrote: "It were far better to sail forever in the light of blindness with sense and feeling and mind, than to be content with the mere act of seeing. The only lightless dark is the night of darkness in ignorance and insensibility."

~ *God of light, we thank Thee for the gift of sight. Tenderly bless those who have it not, and give us all power to see heavenly reality. Amen.*

A strong man with an incurable disease.

> . . . my strength is made perfect in weakness. Most gladly therefore will I rather glory in my infirmities, that the power of Christ may rest upon me. (II Corinthians 12:9)

Physical suffering seems to have been Paul's lot throughout

much of his life. An eye affliction caused pain and impaired his sight. Illness sometimes made him delay journeys. He speaks of his physical weakness and unimposing appearance. Yet he had to endure beatings, imprisonment, stonings, and exposure. At least once he seems to have felt that God answered: "My grace is sufficient for thee: my strength is made perfect in weakness." Rather than forgetting him, God was using suffering to bless him with a greater measure of His strength.

Father of all who suffer, we pray for those who are in pain. Where possible within Thy purpose, relieve; where wiser for their good, bless them through their suffering. Amen.

Consider Toscanini and his fortunate handicap.

> Therefore I take pleasure in infirmities, in reproaches, in necessities, in persecutions, in distresses for Christ's sake: for when I am weak, then am I strong. (II Corinthians 12:10)

Arturo Toscanini, perhaps the greatest living symphony orchestra conductor, got his great opportunity partly because he was nearsighted. He found it necessary, when he played in the orchestra, to memorize his part, and then he memorized the music of the other instruments. When the director became suddenly ill, Toscanini offered to conduct because he knew all of the music. He received a great ovation, and was made the regular conductor of the orchestra. His handicap had but spurred him to higher attainments. Many of the world's great men and women have had handicaps that proved to be blessings.

Forgive us, our Father, for complaining of our handicaps, and teach us to use them as steppingstones. Amen.

Have you ever been sick in a good cause?

> From henceforth let no man trouble me: for I bear in my body the marks of the Lord Jesus. (Galatians 6:17)

The deafness of Walter Rauschenbusch was at once a handicap and a source of power. It was a badge of his sainthood, both because of the patience with which he endured it and because of its origin. Called on an errand of mercy in midwinter, he left his sickbed in a severe illness and ventured out in a bitter winter storm. The premature exposure cost him his hearing, but with joy unabated he went on with his sacrificial work. No one could note that deafness and ever question the sincerity of the Shepherd of the Tenements.

Forgive, O Christ of Calvary, the lack of evidence of sacrifice on our part in Thy name. Bring us into fellowship with Thy suffering. Amen.

What is it that makes you ill?

Why art thou cast down, O my soul? and why art thou disquieted within me? hope in God: for I shall yet praise him, who is the health of my countenance, and my God. (Psalms 43:5)

C. Jung, in his *Modern Man in Search of a Soul,* wrote: "Among all my patients in the second half of life, that is to say over thirty-five, there has not been one whose problem in the last resort has not been that of finding a religious outlook on life. It is safe to say that every one of them fell ill because he had lost that which the living religions of every age have given to their followers, and not one of them has been really healed who did not regain his religious outlook."

We place our souls in Thy hands, O Thou physician God, that Thou mayest heal our spiritual ills and dispel all of our fears. Amen.

INSECURITY

Advice for the time when the contrary winds blow.

> And he saw them toiling in rowing; for the wind was contrary unto them . . . (Mark 6:48)

Those whom the Master constrains to follow a path of duty frequently find, like the disciples of old, that the "winds are contrary unto them." The breadwinner who labors to support his family sometimes finds the going difficult. Parents who take seriously the task of rearing and training their children discover that there are many contrary winds. Citizens who would serve their communities from high motives encounter adverse blasts. Newly converted Christians may be shocked to find that to follow Christ they must face contrary winds. All who serve and lead in the work of the churches must labor against currents of indifference and even opposition. The disciples met the test of adverse winds in a direct way; they kept on rowing. Jesus watched unseen, drew near in their extremity, responded to their call, and was adequate to their need.

God of life's winds and waves, give us patience to keep rowing when progress seems impossible, and vision to see Thy face in the shadows, keeping watch. We ask it in Jesus' name. Amen.

You can be a saint in Caesar's household.

> All the saints salute you, chiefly they that are of Caesar's household. (Philippians 4:22)

A woman said to me recently, "I should like to become a Christian, but I am in a situation in which it is impossible to live a Christian life." Most of us sometimes feel that our situations make it particularly difficult to follow Christ. If our friends were all practicing Christians, we would have no difficulty. But surely God understands that we must conform to our circumstances. Like a dash of cold water in a sleepy face come to us the words of Paul: "All the saints salute you, chiefly they that are of Caesar's household." Saints in Caesar's household! Surely none of us is in a more difficult situation than that. We can be Christians in spite of everything.

Give us courage, O God, to follow Christ, rather than the crowd. Amen.

When all is turmoil, remember that God is on your side.

> For the Son of man is come to seek and to save that which was lost. (Luke 19:10)

In Jesus' story of the lost sheep, the spotlight is not on the poor, scared sheep, but rather on the shepherd, distressed over the loss of something precious to him. In the story of the coin, the emphasis is not on the lonely coin, but rather on the woman who has lost something valuable. In the story of the prodigal, the point is not the action of the boy, but the compassion of the father. The tragedy of lost souls is not only their misery, but the loss of something precious to and needed by God. People are God's treasures, and He will not lose them if He can prevent it.

O Thou good shepherd of the sheep, teach us to see the infinite value to Thee of one precious soul, and to share Thy holy passion for the redemption of the whole race. Amen.

The only hope in a divided world:

> Glory to God in the highest, and on earth peace, good will toward men. (Luke 2:14)

Peace on earth and good will among men were linked together in the song of the angels when the Saviour was born, and we shall not have one without the other. The popular fallacy that peace is to be attained by one nation becoming so terrible that all others will fear her, will lead inevitably to war. To say of any people, "The only language they can understand is force," is to deny the faith of Jesus, to despair of peace, and to confess our own lack of good will.

Search us, O God, in the light of Thy cross to see if we desire peace, and convict us if we be enemies of the Prince of Peace. Amen.

How to live with an H-bomb.

> For the mountains shall depart, and the hills be removed; but my kindness shall not depart from thee, neither shall the covenant of my peace be removed, saith the Lord that hath mercy on thee. (Isaiah 54:10)

Dr. J. Robert Oppenheimer, director of the Institute for Advanced Study, has said: "Above all we must realize how long a pull is ahead of us. For men of our times will never have a sense of security again." The Bible has always told us of the beginning and end of the world. The difference is that the vivid descriptions of the end have ceased to be a vision, and have become physics. Christianity started in a world seen to be crumbling. The consummation of the kingdom has always been beyond time, and not one principle or promise of the Bible is shaken by the atomic bomb.

We thank Thee, eternal God, for foundations for our faith that can stand being shaken. We pray that the precariousness of our time may turn men's minds to the things that endure. Amen.

Whom is God for, if not the needy?

> The sacrifices of God are a broken spirit: a broken and a contrite heart, O God, thou wilt not despise. (Psalms 51:17)

As a water carrier goes to the well, not because his vessel is full, but because it is empty, so we pray, not because we are good or strong or wise, but because we are needy. In his great little volume called *Prayer,* Dr. O. Hallesby says: "To pray is nothing more involved than to let Jesus into our needs. To pray is to give Jesus permission to employ His powers in the alleviation of our distress."

For our weakness, Lord, give us strength; for our blindness, light; for our sin, forgiveness; for our every need, Thy full supply. Amen.

A little bit of faith removes a lot of uncertainty.

> Thy shoes shall be iron and brass; and as thy days, so shall thy strength be. (Deuteronomy 33:25)

To Asher's tribe Moses spoke. One would not need iron shoes to walk on velvet. So the promise was a warning that rugged pathways lay ahead, and the assurance that no experience would come to them for which God would not prepare them. He added: "As thy days, so shall thy strength be." Each day would bring its own strength. The iron shoes would be forged of the ore in the very rocks over which they would walk.

We have learned, Father God, that rugged pathways await us all, and that grace, like daily bread, is given day by day. We trust Thee for strength when we need it. Amen.

A lesson in vital mathematics:

> I can do all things through Christ which strengtheneth me.
> (Philippians 4:13)

Faith in God is the fountain source of true faith in ourselves. J. B. Tidwell was born in poverty, of ignorant, law-evading parents. He was converted and longed for what seemed impossible: an education. Someone gave him a motto by which he lived the rest of his years: "J. B. Tidwell plus God equals enough." As Bible teacher at Baylor University he inspired tens of thousands of students. Paul wrote from prison: "I can do all things through Christ which strengtheneth me."

We do not ask, O God, for tasks commensurate with our strength, but for strength commensurate with our tasks. Amen.

Uncertainty is only a lack of knowledge.

> For now we see through a glass, darkly; but then face to face: now I know in part; but then shall I know even as also I am known. (I Corinthians 13:12)

A traveler in the Orient stood for a long time watching a weaver at work on a rug. Though he used threads of many colors, there was no discernible pattern, and innumerable loose ends marred the appearance of the work. But finally the weaver finished his task, trimmed off the loose threads, and turned the rug over to display a gorgeous and perfect pattern. So does God's providence in our lives seem but a hodgepodge of loose threads. But when we see it from above we shall discern the pattern.

We do not ask to understand the event of our lives, Master, but that Thy hand shall weave the pattern, and that we may one day see as Thou seest. Amen.

Perhaps you're trying to do more than your share.

> Give us this day our daily bread. (Matthew 6:11)

An English scientist once calculated all the forces responsible for producing a corn crop and assigned to each item of creative energy a percentage value. He computed a share of credit for preparation of the soil, planting, cultivating, and harvesting the crop. The soil's fertility, the grain's power to germinate, and such helpful influences as air, rain, and sun were taken into account. He arranged the ratios in two columns, with God's work in one and man's work in the other. The result of his trial balance showed the crop to be 7 per cent the result of man's efforts and 93 per cent the work of God.

Our provident Father, not as mere sentiment, but recognizing our complete dependence on Thee, we pray: Give us this day our daily bread. We ask this in His name. Amen.

Some of us weren't ready for a gale.

> My voice shalt thou hear in the morning, O Lord; in the morning will I direct my prayer unto thee, and will look up. (Psalms 5:3)

Before beginning to play an overture, the musicians in an orchestra must tune their instruments. A wise traveler, before starting on an automobile trip, will consult road maps, fill his tank with gasoline, and check the lubrication system of his machine. An early morning quiet time with God gives us opportunity to harmonize our spirits with the eternal, to orient ourselves by His compass, to take on spiritual fuel, and to discover and remedy points of destructive friction within us.

We remember, Father, that our Master rose up very early to commune with Thee. Remind us to begin each day with prayer. Amen.

Be critical.

> And they were all amazed, and were in doubt, saying one to another, What meaneth this? (The Acts 2:12)

At Pentecost those who had learned to believe had to learn first to doubt. "And they were all amazed, and were in doubt." They had been sure of themselves, but when their beliefs were challenged by a new gospel, they turned critically on their former faith. Some did not doubt. But the receptive minds were those that doubted. Had Saul of Tarsus not doubted his former faith, he would not have been converted. Had Nicodemus not doubted the old law, he would not have come to Jesus. We need to learn to doubt some of the shibboleths of our day.

Master, teach us to be honest doubters of that which needs criticism, and unreserved in our commitment to that which we believe. Amen.

The tragedies of life's orange peelings:

> But Peter said unto him, Although all shall be offended, yet
> will not I. (Mark 14:29)

Jesus warned His disciples, during the night of His betrayal,
that all would be offended because of Him. One of them,
Simon Peter, was especially sure that he would not. Yet he
was the one who denied his Lord. Bobby Leach, an Englishman, went over Niagara Falls without serious harm. Some
years later he was walking on the street, slipped on an orange
peeling, and was taken to the hospital with a badly fractured
leg. He feared Niagara, and took every precaution for safety.
He paid no attention to the orange peeling, and it caused his
fall.

*⮕ Knowing our weakness, Lord, we pray for Thy sustain-
ing hand every moment of life. Save us from temptations that
take us unawares. Amen.*

Today's missed opportunity sows the seeds for tomorrow's.

> Then said the woman, Whom shall I bring up unto thee?
> And he said, Bring me up Samuel. (I Samuel 28:11)

For many years Samuel tried to get Saul to heed wise counsel,
but the king was headstrong and would not listen. Then the
old prophet died, and the ancient enemy came upon Israel.
What to do? To the witch of Endor hastened Saul to beg her
to call Samuel back that he might listen to him. The privilege
he had spurned for years he now sought. Through the ages
all the sages have warned of the folly of that. Each day's opportunities must be grasped as they come.

*⮕ Lord of our lives, Thou art the God who goeth ever for-
ward. Teach us to live each moment at its best, to grasp
today's opportunities, and keep our faces toward the future.
Amen.*

Reassuring words from the most-loved psalm.

> The Lord is my shepherd; I shall not want. (Psalms 23:1)

Because the Lord is my shepherd, I shall not lack for anything. Do I need rest? "He maketh me to lie down in green
pastures." Refreshment? "He leadeth me beside the still
waters." Restoration? "He restoreth my soul." Guidance? "He

leadeth me in the paths of righteousness." Protection? ". . . through the valley of the shadow of death . . . thou art with me." Food? "Thou preparest a table before me . . ." Balm? "Thou anointest my head with oil . . ." What more could I ask? ". . . goodness and mercy shall follow me all the days of my life: and I will dwell in the house of the Lord for ever."

Blessed shepherd of our souls, we trust Thee for all things, and follow gladly wherever Thou shalt lead us. Amen.

Do you feel as if God were too far away?

> I will not leave you comfortless: I will come to you. Yet a little while, and the world seeth me no more; but ye see me: because I live, ye shall live also. (John 14:18, 19)

The greatest fact of Christian experience is the presence of the living Lord with the believer. Saintly Phillips Brooks once said: "All experience grows more and more to be the pressure of His life on ours. He is here; I know Him; He knows me. It is no figure of speech, it is the realest thing in the world, and every day it grows realer, until one wonders with delight what it will grow to as the years go on."

Grant us, blessed friend and guide, a sense of Thy presence so vivid that Thou shalt be indeed closer to us than breathing, nearer than hands and feet. Amen.

Or perhaps you're not doing all that you should be doing.

> But know this, that if the goodman of the house had known in what watch the thief would come, he would have watched, and would not have suffered his house to be broken up. (Matthew 24:43)

During the War of the Spanish Succession in 1704, a combined British and Dutch fleet bombarded Gibraltar for several days with no effect. When Saints' Day came, the Spanish soldiers went to church to pray against the heretic besiegers. British sailors ascended the rock at a place that would have been inaccessible had the Spaniards been alert. The pious garrison came out from their prayers to find the fortress in the hands of the English, who have kept it ever since. Piety without vigilance lost Gibraltar.

Save us, O God, from hypocrisy, pride, censoriousness, and all the sins which slip so insidiously into pious hearts. Amen.

Are you availing yourself of life's road map?

> If any man will do his will, he shall know of the doctrine, whether it be of God, or whether I speak of myself. (John 7:17)

A man who had never ventured beyond the borders of his home country planned a trip to California. A friend gave him a road map and taught him how to read it. Doubtful at first, he decided to try to follow it. Before the first half day was gone his doubts had passed, for scores of confirmations were appearing to make him know the map was accurate. So Christ offers us a way of life. We may doubt it, but if we follow for even a day we discover that He is the way.

Guide of our lives, we have walked with Thee long enough to know we can trust Thee. Lead Thou on, and we will follow without fear. Amen.

Learn the benefits of filling your shelves.

> And I gave my heart to seek and search out by wisdom concerning all things that are done under heaven . . . (Ecclesiastes 1:13)

The men and women who have been the greatest benefactors of the race have fed on great ideas. Discoverers and inventors have been those with the "hungry mind." A recent study shows that the states spending the most money per pupil for public education also produce the largest number of top-flight men of science. As the author of the book of Ecclesiastes discovered, the quest for knowledge is not the ultimate good, but a well-stocked mind is essential for accurate thinking. Through reading, listening, observing, and meditating, we fill the empty shelves of our minds with goods.

God, who hast made our minds hungry for truth and hast created truth for their hunger, teach us to discern what things are important and to discover and live by them. We ask it in the name of our Teacher. Amen.

Four ways, and only one offers contentment.

> For to me to live is Christ, and to die is gain. (Philippians 1:21)

There are four things that a man can do with life. He can run away from it, like Jonah. He can run along with it, like one of the crowd who shouted, "Crucify him!" He can take hold of life with his own plan and purpose and run it to good account. Or he can put his life into the hands of one greater than himself, and let Him run it. It was plain common sense that Dwight L. Moody used in expressing: "Let God have your life; He can do more with it than you can."

Thou who hast made us for a purpose, help us to know the goal of our living and guide us to it. Amen.

It rains on the just and unjust, but the just have umbrellas.

Enter ye in at the strait gate: for wide is the gate, and broad is the way, that leadeth to destruction . . . (Matthew 7:13)

In the story of the foundations, with which Jesus closed the Sermon on the Mount, both types of builders had heard His word, and both approved. Then both had the houses of their lives tested by life's storms. One, however, had basic strength to meet the test, while the other did not. The difference between Christians and those without Christ, is not in the difficulties they face, but rather in the resources they have with which to face them.

Father, we do not ask to be excused from the buffetings of life's storms; we ask for strength to endure them. Amen.

Your mighty fortress lies within you.

Not that I speak in respect of want: for I have learned, in whatsoever state I am, therewith to be content. (Philippians 4:11)

King Henry VI, to the rest of the quotation cited above, adds: "My crown is in my heart not on my head." The secret of Paul's contentment was a conviction that his life was in the hands of a God who would supply his every need, and who had a purpose in everything that happened to him. Even his imprisonment was "for the defence of the gospel," and each thing that happened to him fell out "unto the furtherance of the gospel." Even a thorn in the flesh was for the purpose of demonstrating Christ's grace.

Having learned that the world cannot give contentment, we seek the peace that comes through life in harmony with Thy will, through Jesus, our Lord. Amen.

The two most assuring words in our language:

Are not two sparrows sold for a farthing? and one of them shall not fall on the ground without your Father. (Matthew 10:29)

This story is told by Dr. W. H. Houghton of Moody Institute: "Somewhere along the New England coast there is a simple little gravestone which has on it two words, 'God knows.' Many years ago a baby's body was washed ashore from a wreck. The baby was nameless, so far as human identification was concerned. The simple, direct confidence of the New Englanders was expressed in the two words on the stone." In an age that tends to consider human beings as only statistics, we need to be taken back to the Bible assurance that God knows our names.

✎ *Eternal Father, we sometimes feel that we are utterly insignificant in this great world in Thine immense universe. Give us anew the assurance that we are Thy dear children. Amen.*

And always, look to the stars.

Jesus Christ the same yesterday, and to day, and for ever. (Hebrews 13:8)

To say, "Jesus Christ the same yesterday, and to day, and for ever," means more than simply that there is a person who does not change. That person is He by whom all things were made, and without whom nothing was made. In Him all things consist. Everything material is changing constantly. Human beings are being born, growing, aging, and dying. Earthly institutions are rising, declining, and disappearing. But the most impressive fact is not change, but stability. That which is founded in the nature of God is eternal. Righteousness, love, and truth pass not away.

✎ *Eternal God, who changest all, but art Thyself unchanging, above all blessings we thank Thee for Thyself, in whom we live and move and have our being. Amen.*

SUSPICION AND MISTRUST

The old one about sticks and stones.

> . . . let him alone, and let him curse; for the Lord hath bidden him. (II Samuel 16:11)

Shimei, a kinsman of the discredited King Saul, met David and his retinue, loudly cursed the young king, and threw stones at him and his friends. Abishai, one of the guards, asked permission to turn aside and take off the head of the disturber. But David said, "Let him curse." It is rarely worth while for us to defend ourselves against the raillery or criticism of others. Let us be concerned about God's opinion of us, and if men will curse us, let them curse.

Father, we thank Thee for criticism. May we be wiser by accepting that which is valid, and more patient by enduring that which is unjust. Amen.

Murder has a family tree.

> Thou shalt not kill. (Exodus 20:13)

Human life is sacred. God forbids killing directly, as did Cain when he slew his brother, or by proxy, as did David when he murdered Uriah. He forbids suicide, for "ye are not your own," and does not permit needless physical risks or dissipation that kills by degrees. As Jesus interpreted it, anger that would prompt a blow, smoldering hatred, and even contempt for the worth of the life of another that would make us careless of his safety, are murderous in God's sight.

Deliver Thy world, O God, from the crime and tragedy of war, and guide those who seek means of removing its causes. Amen.

Here's what happens when you hate someone.

> But if ye forgive not men their trespasses, neither will your Father forgive your trespasses. (Matthew 6:15)

Dr. Harry Emerson Fosdick says: "Hating people is like burning down your house to get rid of a rat." Harboring ill will occasionally results in some harm to the person against whom it is held, but it always causes great damage to the one who holds it. It destroys happiness, injures the personality, and blights the religious life. Jesus said: "But if ye forgive not men their trespasses, neither will your Father forgive your trespasses." Gautama, the founder of Buddhism, said that it is an eternal rule that hatred does not cease by hatred, but only by love.

Our prayer today, Father of us all, is that men and nations may learn the folly of hatred and the power of love. Amen.

"He doesn't belong to my club, you see."

> And John answered and said, Master, we saw one casting out devils in thy name; and we forbad him, because he followeth not with us.
> And Jesus said unto him, Forbid him not: for he that is not against us is for us. (Luke 9:49, 50)

John expressed an attitude which has troubled the Church for ages and is its scandal now: "We forbad him [to work in Jesus' name], because he followeth not with us." It is still fatally easy for us to confound the cause of Christ with that of our particular group. The master announced a timeless principle to determine the policy of the Church toward so-called schismatics: "He that is not against us is for us." Welcome the service that anyone renders in Jesus' name, by whatever name he may be called.

O Thou who didst pray that Thine own should be one, we pray for that unity to come, and for deliverance from the impatience with others that postpones its coming. Amen.

Go easy on those you judge.

> . . . for wherein thou judgest another, thou condemnest thyself; for thou that judgest doest the same things. (Romans 2:1)

In some ways we have to judge each other. Executives must form opinions about the ability and also the moral and spiritual qualities of those with whom they work. We are told to be discriminating concerning our teachers. We must be selective in the choice of mates, friends, and business associates. Yet it is disastrous when we set ourselves up as God to judge the worth of those around us. Being without complete knowledge, we inevitably judge unfairly. The result is to set us against our fellow man rather than for him, and to cause us to excuse in ourselves greater faults than those we condemn in others.

Our wise Father who knowest all hearts, make us to be merciless in our judgments upon ourselves and charitable toward all others. Amen.

Don't fence in suspicion.

A soft answer turneth away wrath: but grievous words stir up anger. (Proverbs 15:1)

A trade paper tells of a man who bought a farm and soon afterward met his next-door neighbor, who immediately asked, "Have you bought that farm?" "Yes." "Well, you've bought a lawsuit." "How so?" "Well, sir, I claim your fence is ten feet on my side, and I'm going to court to prove it." "Oh, don't do that," said the new owner, "if the fence is on your side of the line, we'll just move it back." "Do you mean that?" asked the neighbor. "Of course I do," was the reply. "Well, then," said the neighbor, "the fence stays where it is."

Master, we have been very slow to learn the wisdom of the second mile. Teach us to radiate and create in others a spirit of good will. Amen.

Do you look inward or outward?

. . . He that is without sin among you, let him first cast a stone . . . (John 8:7)

My neighbor, who rarely attends church services, tells me that when he does go he sits in the front pew so that he will not be disturbed by seeing the hypocrites in front of him. Most of us who worship regularly feel ourselves to be so much in need of forgiveness that we are not qualified to judge the other sinners around us. The men who were ready to throw stones at a poor, sinful woman stole away ashamed when Jesus uncovered their own guilt. It has been well said that he who lives until he is stoned to death by one without faults will be immortal.

Forgive, kind Father, our hidden and recognized sins, and give us a spirit of love and charity toward all others. Amen.

Do you hoard resentment?

> For if ye forgive men their trespasses, your heavenly Father will also forgive you. (Matthew 6:14)

Vengeance is considered by some people a sacred duty. They feel that to surrender to ill will is a sign of weakness, and they are a little ashamed when they forgive a wrong. Resentment, however, ought to be thrown away as one would dispose of garbage. Imagine a housewife who took pride in never letting any of her kitchen waste be carried away! It would become offensive and her home unpleasant. So does the life become which allows ill will to accumulate.

Have mercy, O God of love, upon all misguided souls who cling to animosity, and teach us the divine art of forgiving. Amen.

A humorous story with a serious point.

> Or how wilt thou say to thy brother, Let me pull out the mote out of thine eye; and, behold, a beam is in thine own eye? (Matthew 7:4)

Jesus painted a picture, half humorous but all true, of a man trying to pick a tiny sliver of wood from the eye of his friend, while a big piece of timber projected from his own eye. So, he said, is the man who, in spite of all his own faults, undertakes to sit in judgment on his neighbor. All of us have a tendency to think of others as the sinners and ourselves as paragons of virtue. It is more profitable, suggests the Master, for us to give more attention to our own shortcomings, that we may be better qualified to help our neighbors.

O Thou who art so patient with us, we pray for clear vision to see our own faults, and charity to overlook the shortcomings of others. Amen.

Must righteousness wear a long face?

> Blessed are they which do hunger and thirst after righteousness: for they shall be filled.
> Blessed are the merciful: for they shall obtain mercy. (Matthew 5:6, 7)

On the Mount, when Jesus had said, "Blessed are they which do hunger and thirst after righteousness," he added immediately, "Blessed are the merciful." As Dr. E. Stanley Jones has observed, "Most righteous people are not merciful toward the failings and shortcomings of others. Their very passion for righteousness makes them hard." However, nothing is more beautiful than the countenance of righteousness when their glistens upon it the tear of mercy.

Save us, Lord, from the hardness of righteousness without mercy, and from the mushiness of mercy without righteousness. Amen.

An object lesson on being critical of others.

And why beholdest thou the mote that is in thy brother's eye, but considerest not the beam that is in thine own eye? (Matthew 7:3)

A lecturer once began his address by tacking a square of white paper on the blackboard. Then he took a piece of crayon and carefully make a black spot in the center of the paper. "Now," he asked, "what do you see?" Person after person answered, "I see a black dot." Finally the lecturer asked, "Don't any of you see a large square of white paper?" So we are prone to ignore the customary good conduct of others and focus on the rare fault.

Master, teach us to discover in every person all of the good traits that are seen by the one who loves that person most. Amen.

The better way to look at resentment.

But I say unto you, Love your enemies, bless them that curse you, do good to them that hate you, and pray for them which despitefully use you, and persecute you. (Matthew 5:44)

A friend in public office approached Sir Eardley Wilmot one day with a complaint that he had been grossly wronged by a fellow official. "Don't you think it would be manly to resent this offense?" he asked. "Yes," replied Sir Eardley, "it would doubtless be manly to resent it, but it would be godlike to forget it." The man's anger cooled, and he decided to forgive and forget.

O Thou who hast forgiven us so much, make us to be so much like Thee that to forgive will be the natural impulse of our hearts. Amen.

Who are the victims of anger?

> Therefore because the king's commandment was urgent, and the furnace exceeding hot, the flame of the fire slew those men that took up Shadrach, Meshach, and Abednego. (Daniel 3:22)

In his fury at the Hebrew youths, Nebuchadnezzar commanded that the furnace into which he would throw them should be heated seven times more than it was wont to be heated. Strangely, however, the objects of his wrath were unhurt, while those who cast them in were killed. Usually the victims of anger or resentment are not the ones against whom it is directed, but rather those who harbor it.

O Thou who dost forgive us so often and so much, teach us to forgive those who trespass against us, whether the injury be real or imagined. Amen.

When everyone appears dishonest, maybe you need new glasses.

> Judge not, that ye be not judged. (Matthew 7:1)

How persistently we set ourselves up as judges of each other, and yet how unfitted we are to judge! Our judgments are biased by our own faults. Either we condemn the sins that we do not care for, and excuse those that we enjoy, or else we censure unmercifully the very things which our consciences condemn in ourselves. Our motives in judging others are never pure. Usually we condemn them in order to build up our own ego.

Forgive us, O Thou righteous judge, for having set ourselves up in Thy seat. Make us merciless in judging our own faults, and charitable in dealing with others. Amen.

Don't throw all your doubts out the window.

> Then saith he to Thomas, Reach hither thy finger, and behold my hands; and reach hither thy hand, and thrust it into my side: and be not faithless, but believing. (John 20:27)

Not all doubting is bad. There are two kinds of fools: one doubts everything, the other nothing. The height of one's mind may be indicated by the length of shadow it casts. He who has never questioned his beliefs has never thought seriously.

Faith is not opposed to reason in the New Testament; it is opposed to sight. We believe, not in that which is unreasonable, but in that which is invisible. He who comes to Christ with the sincere devotion and honest questions of Thomas will find Him ready to lead him into truth.

❧ *God of truth, Thou hast given us our minds, and so dost understand them. Give us spiritual attitudes that will lead to clearer thinking rather than to confusion. Amen.*

LACK OF MONEY AND POSSESSIONS

Is it true that money isn't everything?

> For we brought nothing into this world, and it is certain we can carry nothing out.
> And having food and raiment let us be therewith content.
> (I Timothy 6:7, 8)

By our standards Jesus lived in poverty. Yet, because He wanted no more, He was rich. His quest was not for added possessions, but for opportunities to share what He had. He who has a crust of bread and is happy to share it with another is wealthy. He who has millions and covets more millions is poor. To have nothing is no guarantee that we shall be free from the tyranny of things, but neither will riches bring contentment. There is a minimum of material goods required for the good life, but real living is impossible for him who makes material gain his goal.

➤ Father, we thank Thee for our daily bread. We remember that those who lived the greatest lives this earth has known had less than we. We pray for spiritual riches. Amen.

What you get for nothing may not be a bargain after all.

> And he cast down the pieces of silver in the temple, and departed, and went and hanged himself. (Matthew 27:5)

It is said that for everything we get we must sell something. For my salary I sell a bit of my life, my time, and strength. I sell a piece of property for an agreed price. I have given up the property and received the money. But the most costly gain is that which I get for nothing. If I cheat or fail to pay a debt, I have sold my conscience, my credit, my good name.

➤ Save us, O God, from the folly of selling that which is priceless. Amen.

You can't have anything without sharing it.

> Then Peter said, Silver and gold have I none; but such as I have give I thee . . . (The Acts 3:6)

When Peter said to the beggar at the Gate Beautiful, "Such as I have give I," he stated an inescapable law of life. We cannot have anything without sharing it sooner or later. This is true of material things and also of spiritual qualities. If I have faith, I give faith to others. If I have kindness, I share it with my neighbors. If I have righteousness, they share it. On the other hand, if I have fears or ill will or vices, others will become infected by them. If I would give to the world something noble, I must have nobility within. If I would avoid spreading evil, I must rid my own heart of it.

❧ *O Thou sharing God, we thank Thee for the good things given us by others. Grant that we may keep within us only that which is worthy to be shared. Amen.*

Here's what happened to others:

> If thou seest the oppression of the poor, and violent perverting of judgment and justice in a province, marvel not at the matter: for he that is higher than the highest regardeth; and there be higher than they. (Ecclesiastes 5:8)

A survey made by the American Legion of five hundred veterans in Detroit showed that their VJ Day dreams had failed to materialize. The average veteran had hoped for a home, a new car, five suits, $483 a month, and $1900 in the bank. Instead, he rented a house for $52 a month, and he had a 1939 car, two suits, $311 a month, and $160 in the bank. Interesting; but more interesting is the disillusion of those who have spent their lives realizing their dreams of material things and discover at last that these are not worth what they cost.

❧ *We thank Thee, O Thou giver of all things, for material blessings. We pray that no amount of prosperity may cause us to feel that temporal things are of more value than those that are eternal. Amen.*

Is there anything you'd rather be than rich?

> He that believeth on him is not condemned: but he that believeth not is condemned already, because he hath not believed in the name of the only begotten Son of God. (John 3:18)

A resident of Leeds was so deeply impressed by the sermons of Spurgeon that he willed most of his large estate to him, leaving his own needy relatives poorly provided for. Immediately Spurgeon sent for a lawyer and distributed the entire bequest among the needy relatives. A newspaper writer commented, "Mr. Spurgeon has preached many great sermons, but none more striking than this. He would rather be just than rich." The most effective witnessing for Christ is to show a truly Christian spirit in practical affairs.

❬ *Keep us loyal to Thy gospel, dear Master, in the most eloquent sermons we preach—our daily lives. Amen.*

A twenty-five-cent piece can hide God.

> For the love of money is the root of all evil: which while some coveted after, they have erred from the faith, and pierced themselves through with many sorrows. (I Timothy 6:10)

Robert Hall was once visited by a man who was offended by something the famous preacher had said in a sermon. Having sized the man up as being obsessed with the love of money, Hall took half a sovereign out of his pocket and, opening the Bible, pointed to the word of God. "Can you see that word?" he asked the man. "Certainly." Then the preacher laid the half sovereign over the word. "Can you see it now?" There was no need to answer.

❬ *Knowing the grief that greed brings to the world, we pray, O God, that silver scales may fall from our eyes, that we may see Thee, and see our brothers. Amen.*

What Fritz Kreisler thought about his money:

> Now we have received, not the spirit of the world, but the spirit which is of God; that we might know the things that are freely given to us of God. (I Corinthians 2:12)

Dale Carnegie quotes Fritz Kreisler as protesting that he does not want credit and does not deserve thanks for his wonderful music. "I was born," says the great artist, "with music in my soul. It was a gift of Providence; I did not acquire it. Therefore I do not even look on the money I earn as something of my own. It is public money, entrusted to me for proper disbursement." The great musician has simply recognized that which is true of everyone. All that we have is given, and we are stewards of it under God, the true owner.

❬ *We thank Thee, O Lord, for trusting us with Thy wealth. Give us wisdom to use it for Thee. We pray it in Jesus' name. Amen.*

Which prayer are you praying today?

> And the younger of them said to his father, Father, give me the portion of goods that falleth to me. And he divided unto them his living.
> . . . make me as one of thy hired servants. (Luke 15:12, 19)

The prodigal son prayed two prayers to his father. When his heart was set on the far country he prayed: "Father give me . . ." But when he had come to himself and was ready to return he made another prayer: "Father, make me . . ." We are prodigal sons if our only words to our Father are, "Give me." We begin to be true sons if we kneel before Him and humbly say, "Make me."

❞ *Our prayer to Thee today, good Father, is not for any gift to us, but only that Thou wilt take us and make us fit for Thine own use. Amen.*

Here's what money can't do.

> Thou shalt not covet thy neighbour's house, thou shalt not covet thy neighbour's wife, nor his manservant, nor his maidservant, nor his ox, nor his ass, nor any thing that is thy neighbour's. (Exodus 20:17)

The Ten Commandments end, where Jesus began, with inner motives. "The love of money," says Paul, "is the root of all evil," and money stands for all we covet. From covetousness, people lie, steal, commit adultery, kill, dishonor parents, break the Sabbath, take God's name in vain, and make things their idols and their gods. Only the love of Christ can banish covetousness from the heart.

❞ *Good Father, we would love Thee with heart and mind and soul and strength, that evil may be banished from our affections. Amen.*

The priceless secret of being content.

> Let your conversation be without covetousness; and be content with such things as ye have: for he hath said, I will never leave thee, nor forsake thee. (Hebrews 13:5)

Socrates used to say that contentment is natural wealth, and luxury is artificial poverty. Two centuries later the Roman Plautus declared: "If you are content, you have enough to live upon with comfort." In the same vein the author of the

Epistle to the Hebrews says: "Let your conversation be without covetousness; and be content with such things as ye have." How to be content? Trust God! "For He hath said, I will never leave thee, nor forsake thee."

❧ *Save us, Lord, from being content with ourselves, but give us the true riches of contentment with what we have. Amen.*

Did you know that not all misers have money?

And he said unto them, Take heed, and beware of covetousness: for a man's life consisteth not in the abundance of the things which he possesseth. (Luke 12:15)

When a Christian becomes rich, God either gains a fortune or loses a son. Wealth is a blessing if it is but added power for the service of God; a curse if it displaces God. To the Christian, possessions are a trust to be administered for good. It is said that Mammon is the largest slaveholder in the world, but not all his slaves are rich. One may sell one's soul for a million dollars or for a few pennies. Avarice is not a vice in proportion to riches; it is an attitude toward them.

❧ *Father God, help us to be faithful stewards of our own possessions, and save us from jealousy of those to whom more is entrusted. Amen.*

Eight million dollars couldn't save him from himself.

. . . Is not the life more than meat, and the body than raiment? (Matthew 6:25)

Ivar Kreuger, the Swedish match king who cheated the bankers of the United States alone out of $250 million in the 1920's, through fraudulent financial statements and forged bonds, spent more on himself than any other modern man. From 1918 until his death, the living expenses of this bachelor, who maintained seven city homes, three country estates, and several yachts, averaged eight million dollars a year. Did he find peace and happiness? By 1932 his life had become unbearable to him, and he committed suicide in Paris.

❧ *Giver of all good things, we thank Thee for the riches that money cannot buy, and pray to be saved from a perverted sense of values. Amen.*

The mottoes of two men you've heard about:

> And though I bestow all my goods to feed the poor, and though I give my body to be burned, and have not charity, it profiteth me nothing. (I Corinthians 13:3)

It is said of Jesus that "He went about doing good." Moving among sick, sinning, and discouraged people, He had only one plan: to give. Calvary was the utmost in self-giving. That principle of life is the true mark of His followers. Any life is great if it be lived to give—whether it be the gift to the world of his genius by one of the immortals, or the offering of the work of his hands by a humble laborer. Judas had a motto: What I can, I get. But Peter had a better: What I have, I give.

Dear Father, who art the giver of every good gift, we thank Thee for teaching us that life's abiding satisfactions come not from getting but from giving. Amen.

SHAME AND GUILT

The sin of doing nothing:

> . . . Inasmuch as ye have done it unto one of the least of these my brethren, ye have done it unto me. (Matthew 25:40)

As Jesus taught it, the Christian life is an active, positive matter—and negative living is sin. The priest and Levite in the story of the Good Samaritan are censured for one crime: doing nothing. The fig tree was cursed for one fault: producing no fruit. Those on the left at the Judgment were condemned for one thing: seeing human need and not helping. The Master could not have expressed the idea more strongly than to identify Himself with the needy of the earth: "Inasmuch as ye have done it unto one of the least of these my brethren, ye have done it unto me."

Dear God and Father of the compassionate Christ, help us to learn from Him that life consists of serving those who need us. For His sake we ask it. Amen.

Release your guilt by confessing, not by running.

> Therefore now go, lead the people unto the place of which I have spoken unto thee: behold, mine Angel shall go before thee: nevertheless in the day when I visit I will visit their sin upon them. (Exodus 32:34)

In Moses' absence, Aaron molded a golden calf and led the people to worship it. When his brother returned, he disclaimed responsibility: "Thou knowest the people, that they are set on mischief." Someone else was to blame! And concerning the gold: "I cast it into the fire, and there came out this calf." What a coincidence! Who had made the mold? Usually what we call luck is simply that the materials we have prepared are coming out of the molds we have made. While we see our mistakes as the fault of others or of our bad luck, our case is hopeless. Happy is he who sees, confesses, and corrects his faults!

Father God, forgive our tendency to blame our failure on others or on Thee. Give us moral courage to look at ourselves honestly and deal with our faults faithfully. Amen.

Don't be afraid to admit your guilt.

> If we confess our sins, he is faithful and just to forgive us
> our sins, and to cleanse us from all unrighteousness. (I John
> 1:9)

While Governor of Texas, Pat Neff went to the state penitentiary to select a man to be pardoned. Prisoner after prisoner assured the governor that he was really innocent. When about to leave, he noticed a forlorn-looking man and stopped to speak to him. "I suppose you were wrongly convicted," he said. "No," the man answered, "I was guilty, and they let me off light for what I did." That man received the pardon. Later the Governor said, "He was the only man I could pardon, for he was the only one who saw that he had done wrong. He was ready to change. I followed him, and he went straight."

❧ *Our forgiving God, we confess our failure and sin. Help us to see our faults clearly, that we may remedy them. Amen.*

The first step: knowing you are down.

> . . . Woman, where are those thine accusers? hath no man
> condemned thee?
> She said, No man, Lord. And Jesus said unto her, Neither
> do I condemn thee: go, and sin no more. (John 8:10, 11)

Jesus defended an adulterous woman from her self-appointed executioners, but he did not defend adultery. To the self-righteous He was stern, that He might awaken conscience. To the frightened, convicted culprit He was tender, that He might awaken hope. He was always the friend of sinners, not by excusing sin, but by revealing it for what it was and offering forgiveness and help.

❧ *Friend of sinners, we who have failed so often are grateful for forgiveness and another chance. Help, Lord, that we may go and sin no more. Amen.*

Even life's broken pieces may be recast.

> And the vessel that he made of clay was marred in the hand
> of the potter: so he made it again another vessel, as seemed
> good to the potter to make it. (Jeremiah 18:4)

In a clay pit in Jerusalem, in the valley between the upper and lower city, Jeremiah saw a potter fashioning a lump of clay into a lovely form. Just as he was completing it, the work crumbled in the workman's hands, and some of the fragments fell to the ground. He thought the potter would let them go and begin with new clay, but he gathered the broken pieces and began to make them over. So God, although He had failed with His people, would try again. We have the same God. If our lives are marred, our ideals broken, and we are but the shattered bits of what we might have been, we can have another chance. We can be made over.

Thou, O God, art the potter; we, the clay. Our disfigured failures we bring to Thee. Make of them something beautiful and useful to Thee. Amen.

Every man can be as right as he knows how.

> The spirit of man is the candle of the Lord, searching all the inward parts of the belly. (Proverbs 20:27)

The wise author of Proverbs tells us: "The spirit of man is the candle of the Lord." Moffat's translation is clearer: "Man's conscience is the lamp of the Eternal, flashing into his inmost soul." In Milton's *Paradise Lost*, when He creates man, God says: "I will put mine umpire, Conscience, in his breast." Our moral judgments are fallible, but we are accountable under the light given us. The duty to obey conscience is inflexible.

Thou, righteous Father, hast placed within us that which says, "This is right; that is wrong." By Thy grace we shall be obedient to that voice. Amen.

To you who ask: What's it to me?

> Then said Jesus unto his disciples, If any man will come after me, let him deny himself, and take up his cross, and follow me. (Matthew 16:24)

Because he loves, Jesus takes upon Himself the burden of all the world's heartache and guilt. Does anyone suffer? He feels the pain. Does anyone sin? He shares the shame, because one of His own did it. He wants His followers to share His compassion. Our fault is not that we wound others, but that we do not care that they are wounded; not that we rob them, but that we are not concerned that they are robbed; not that we tempt them to sin, but that we weep not over their sins.

Thou whose heart is laid bare on Calvary, make our hearts sensitive to all that concerns our brothers. We pray, Lord, in Jesus' name. Amen.

For those who think up excuses.

> And they all with one consent began to make excuse. The first said unto him, I have bought a piece of ground, and I must needs go and see it: I pray thee have me excused. (Luke 14:18)

Making excuses is an ancient enterprise. When Adam was called to account for eating the forbidden fruit, he blamed it on his wife. When Saul disobeyed God by keeping the cattle of the Amalekites, he had a ready excuse: "The people spared the best . . . to sacrifice unto the Lord." The Jews returning from captivity excused their failure to build a house to worship: "The time is not come." Of those who declined the invitation to the supper, Jesus said, "They all . . . began to make excuse."

O Thou who seest the secrets of our hearts, we confess our disposition to be dishonest even with ourselves. Help us to see our motives clearly, and so to live that we shall not need to make excuses. Amen.

A story about not-doing:

> Therefore to him that knoweth to do good, and doeth it not, to him it is sin. (James 4:17)

Luke's thumbnail biography of Jesus does not say: "He went about not doing any harm," but rather. "He went about doing good." The Golden Rule is not: "Do not to another what you would not want him to do to you," but rather: "All things whatsoever ye would that men should do to you, do ye even so to them." Being a good soldier is not merely refraining from betraying one's cause, but fighting valiantly in that cause. Christian living is not merely refraining from doing harm, but rather it is doing all the good we can in Christ's name.

Convict us of our sin, O God, not so much in the greatness of the harm we do, but in the littleness of the good. Amen.

Those skeletons in your closet!

> So they went, and made the sepulchre sure, sealing the stone, and setting a watch. (Matthew 27:66)

There was something pathetic about the efforts of the Jewish hierarchy to make sure that their disposition of Jesus was final. "Give us a lock and some soldiers," they said, "and He shall not escape." History laughs at their folly. Soldiers and locks were simply irrelevant. Diplomats and statesmen have made agreements and then asked: "Have we enough soldiers to make the tomb secure?" The real question is: "Whom have we crucified?" As individuals we ask: Is the lock strong enough to protect me from the ghost of my past actions? Better to inquire: What have I done to God?

Heavenly Father, teach us the folly of trying to defend or enforce that which is wrong. Give us the vision to see that nothing is strong unless it is right. Amen.

And what about your own housekeeping?

Wash me thoroughly from mine iniquity, and cleanse me from my sin. (Psalms 51:2)

God is a neat housekeeper. When we get away from the areas that man has polluted, we are always impressed with the cleanness of nature. Mountain air and sparkling spring water, the wave-washed sands of the beach, virgin snow on the fields, the freshness of the forests after rain—all remind us of God's cleansing touch. After watching the cleansing rain carry away the dust and bring freshness, let us long for that same God to bring cleansing and freshness to our souls.

Create in me a clean heart, O God, and renew a right spirit within me. Wash me thoroughly from mine iniquity, and cleanse me from my sin. Amen.

Our own lie-detectors!

Which shew the work of the law written in their hearts, their conscience also bearing witness, and their thoughts the mean while accusing or else excusing one another. (Romans 2:15)

Cain, after murdering his brother Abel through jealousy, is represented as having said that everyone who saw him would want to slay him. Conscience does make cowards. The lie-detector mechanism is so constructed as to register one's nervous reactions to one's own suspicion that falsehood cannot be hidden. How foolish to suppose that we can find happiness through wrong! The moral law is written on our hearts.

God of truth, we thank Thee for every evidence of the weakness of wrong and the inevitable triumph of right. Help us to devote ourselves wholly to that which is good. Amen.

How good is a good alibi?

> And the Lord God said unto the woman, What is this that
> thou hast done? And the woman said, The serpent beguiled
> me, and I did eat. (Genesis 3:13)

Marshal Stalin told a story at the Teheran Conference which
caused much laughter, but shows keen insight into human
nature. He said: "The neighbor of an Arab sheik asked for
the loan of a rope. 'I cannot lend it,' replied the sheik, 'for I
need it to tie up my milk with.' 'But surely,' said the other,
'you do not tie up your milk with a rope.' 'Brother,' said the
sheik, 'when you don't want to do something, one reason is as
good as another.' " In Jesus' story of the great supper, the invited guests offered many excuses, but they were made from
one motive: a desire not to attend.

*O Thou who knowest our inward parts, give us right
motives and sincerity in striving to attain them. Amen.*

The bus company can afford it. Can you?

> Thou shalt not steal. (Exodus 20:15)

One after another follow the Commandments safeguarding
life, family, and then property. God is interested not in things,
but in persons, and property is essential to persons. Without
it we cannot survive, and in handling it we develop and ex-
hibit character. To deprive another unjustly of property may
harm him little or much, but it harms the thief irreparably.
The transit company can afford to lose the bus fare I might
fail to pay, but I cannot afford the personality damage of
cheating.

*We accept the things we have as a trust from Thee, our
God. Help us to be faithful and honest stewards. For Jesus'
sake. Amen.*

Have you lost the friend inside of you?

> And herein do I exercise myself, to have always a con-
> science void of offense toward God, and toward men. (The
> Acts 24:16)

While President of the United States, Abraham Lincoln
wrote: "I desire so to conduct the affairs of this administra-
tion that if at the end, when I come to lay down the reins of
power, I have lost every other friend on earth I shall at least

have one friend left, and that friend shall be down inside of me." Paul, the great preacher of God's grace toward sinners, declared before his accusers: "And herein do I exercise myself, to have always a conscience void of offence toward God, and toward men."

❧ *Help us so to live, O God, that we shall have nothing of which to be ashamed. We ask it in Jesus' name. Amen.*

Have you an unpaid account with God?

> I will go into thy house with burnt offerings: I will pay thee my vows,
> Which my lips have uttered, and my mouth hath spoken, when I was in trouble. (Psalms 66:13, 14)

Under the pressure of difficulties the Psalmist had made promises to God, but when the troubles were passed, the promises were forgotten. When he came to the temple to worship he was reminded of his failure to keep them. Then he declared: "I will pay thee my vows, which my lips have uttered, and my mouth hath spoken, when I was in trouble." Many of us have similar unpaid balances in our accounts with God. One of the benefits of worship is to bring to mind these neglected duties.

❧ *We are grateful for every reminder of our unpaid vows to Thee, O God. We now purpose by Thy help to keep our promises. Amen.*

The saddest words: It might have been!

> For I say unto you, That except your righteousness shall exceed the righteousness of the scribes and Pharisees, ye shall in no case enter into the kingdom of heaven. (Matthew 5:20)

Christian living does not mean principally giving up things, but rather adding on things. It is necessary to leave off things which hinder our service, but the motive is positive: to do good. God's children are not merely expected to avoid offending Him, but to serve Him. Brotherhood does not mean refraining from harming people, but rather helping them. Jesus went about doing good. Too often we are content merely to go about.

❧ *O Thou working God, Father of Jesus, who worked, forgive us that we have thought of our calling as negative. Help us to make our lives count for good. Amen.*

The slave who thought he was free.

> Know ye not, that to whom ye yield yourselves servants to obey, his servants ye are . . . whether of sin unto death, or of obedience unto righteousness? (Romans 6:16)

A slave has just left my study. Ironically, he has become a slave through trying to be free. He felt that the Ten Commandments limited his freedom. So he broke them. Man-made laws chafed him, and he violated them, but for several years he was not able to escape the restraints of prison, either. He defied even the laws of physical well-being, and now his health is broken. Not yet has he learned that freedom is to be attained only in harmony with God and His universe!

O Thou infinite God, we thank Thee for the freedom we have found in life surrendered to Thee. Willingly and gladly we offer praise, adoration, and obedience to Thee. Amen.

Why are we sinners?

> If we say that we have no sin, we deceive ourselves . . . (I John 1:8)

Dr. Reinhold Niebuhr has done much to make us realize how completely our human nature is bound up with sin, and how dependent we are on God to redeem us. Even our strong points become occasions for temptation. We are sinners, not because we have killed or committed adultery or stolen, but because we are human and selfish and proud and dishonest. The sins of the successful, respectable, and powerful people may be more vicious than those of the weak. Blessed is he who sees clearly his own sinfulness and confesses his need for redemption.

We throw ourselves upon Thy mercy, blessed Saviour, and trust Thee to perfect the work of redemption which Thou hast begun in us. Amen.

If you see your sins, there's hope for you.

> And he arose, and came to his father. But when he was yet a great way off, his father saw him, and had compassion, and ran, and fell on his neck, and kissed him. (Luke 15:20)

With three stories Jesus taught the lesson of the lost things. A sheep, a coin, and a boy were lost, but in each case the search went on until the last was found. He stated His own mission:

"The Son of Man is come to seek and to save that which is lost." In His eyes, the humble publican standing afar off and with downcast eyes was closer to God than the respected Pharisee cataloguing his virtues. Jesus found it easier to redeem outcasts, publicans, and prostitutes than to overcome the pride of self-righteous men. If we have the mind of Christ, no person in the world is too low for our concern, or for our faith in God's redeeming power.

Teach us, Master, to be diligent in good works, but let them not destroy us because of pride in them. May our hands be always extended to help any who need us! Amen.

Perhaps you took too much for granted.

> But they, supposing him to have been in the company, went a day's journey; and they sought him among their kinsfolk and acquaintance. (Luke 2:44)

Mary and Joseph supposed Jesus to be in the company, but He was not. To live, we must take many things for granted. But it is easy to carry this comfortable way of assuming that all is well into areas where that is not justified. Parents assume that their children are equipped to live without spiritual training. Christians suppose others will do the work of the churches. Citizens suppose that someone will take care of the necessary civic activities of their communities. People without spiritual foundations suppose that somehow things will work out all right. Night came, and the boy Jesus was missing. Life has a way of calling us to face our unjustified supposings. Some of us will go back, sorrowing, to make amends. We may find the answer at the house of God. But every day sad souls discover that they have taken things for granted too long. It is wise for us occasionally to re-examine the things we take for granted.

Heavenly Father, if in anything we are assuming that all is well when it is not, show us our lack, and lead us to recover what we have missed. Amen.

Do you really want peace of mind?

> And forgive us our debts, as we forgive our debtors. (Matthew 6:12)

We are unfair to God when we keep begging for that which He offers freely. Judas went out and hanged himself, not because Jesus would not forgive him, but because he would not accept forgiveness. Many people torture themselves with remorse, not because God will not give peace, but because they have not accepted it. Prayer should not be merely imploring hands pleading with God, but receptive hands stretched out to accept the gift He proffers.

Father, we believe Thou dost offer us forgiveness and peace, and we accept them gratefully from Thy hand. Amen.

Kipling was dead wrong here.

For verily I say unto you, Till heaven and earth pass, one jot or one tittle shall in no wise pass from the law, till all be fulfilled. (Matthew 5:18)

Kipling wrote: "Ship me somewhere east of Suez, where the best is like the worst, where there ain't no Ten Commandments, and a man can raise a thirst." Most of us have felt at some time that we should like to escape from moral restraints, but the Ten Commandments are not local laws. A minister walking across a prison yard passed a convict breaking up stones, and remarked that the prisoner still had a lot of work to do. "Yes," agreed the convict. "These stones are like the Ten Commandments: you can go on breaking them, but you can never get rid of them."

Forever, O Lord, Thy Word is settled in heaven. Incline our hearts to perform Thy statutes always, even unto the end. Amen.

One sin at the bottom of many others.

Wherefore putting away lying, speak every man truth with his neighbour: for we are members one of another. (Ephesians 4:25)

Freud is the great modern exposer of self-deceit as man's commonest and stupidest sin, if not his only sin. Dr. Richard C. Cabot published an excellent book in 1938 called *Honesty*. In it he says: "Lying is the king of vices. Almost all man's disgraces are instrumented by deceit." On the other hand he declares: "Honesty, then, is the king of all virtues." He who is basically dishonest is capable of any wrong, but one who is scrupulously honest has the essential foundation for building the finest character.

O Thou who canst not lie, we do not believe Thou dost want us to lie. Help us to think and speak the truth. Amen.

But you have to live with yourself.

> From that time forth began Jesus to shew unto his disciples, how that he must go unto Jerusalem, and suffer many things of the elders and chief priests and scribes, and be killed, and be raised again the third day.
> Then Peter took him, and began to rebuke him, saying, Be it far from thee, Lord: this shall not be unto thee. (Matthew 16:21, 22)

Whatever else the cross of Christ may mean, it surely proves His integrity. Worldly-wise Peter saw no necessity for it, and admonished Him to put it out of His mind. In the court of Caiaphas he proved that a man can save his skin by telling a little lie. A compromising Christ would not have been killed. Compromising Christians are not persecuted. But after Peter had learned sincerity from his crucified Master, he could neither be swayed nor silenced.

Thy cross, O Christ, rebukes us who save our skins at any cost. Help us to attain the sincerity that makes martyrs faithful unto death. Amen.

Did you choose the wrong way?

> For the good that I would I do not: but the evil which I would not, that I do. (Romans 7:19)

Portia, in Shakespeare's *Merchant of Venice,* reflecting on her own weakness, added, "I can easier teach twenty what were good to be done, than to be one of the twenty to follow my own teaching." In the Epistle to the Romans, Paul argued that even the most benighted heathen had more knowledge of right and wrong than he practiced. And he insisted that his own need was not a clearer knowledge of the right, but power to enable him to choose the right that he knew.

We pray, dear God, not only for light to walk by, but for a transformation of our perverse wills that will make us choose the right way. Amen.

Are you sorry you pretended you were someone else?

> That ye may approve things that are excellent; that ye may be sincere and without offence . . . (Philippians 1:10)

The sharpest words of condemnation Jesus ever spoke were addressed to people who were insincere. He gave to the language a word to describe them: "hypocrite." It means an actor who wears a mask and plays a part. Jesus recognized the prevalence of pretense, particularly among religious people, and the great harm done by it. His followers had to be transparently honest with themselves, their fellows, and their heavenly Father.

❧ *Our understanding Father, Thou knowest how readily we assume an actor's part, even when we pray. Teach us, though it be painful and low, to be sincere. In Jesus' name. Amen.*

The battlefield within the human heart.

> I find then a law, that, when I would do good, evil is present with me. (Romans 7:21)

An Indian received a package at a trading post with a silver coin caught in the wrapping paper. The next day he returned the coin to the surprised trader. The Indian explained: "I got good man and bad man in my heart. The good man says, 'It is not yours'; the bad man says, 'Nobody will know.' The good man say, 'Take it back'; the bad man say, 'Never mind.' So I think I go to sleep, but the good man and the bad man talk all night and disturb me."

❧ *Lord Christ, who in the wilderness didst face temptation and overcome it, teach us to heed the voice of duty, and to turn away from the appeal of wrong. Amen.*

Are you looking only for a patch?

> And he spake also a parable unto them; No man putteth a piece of a new garment upon an old; if otherwise, then both the new maketh a rent, and the piece that was taken out of the new agreeth not with the old. (Luke 5:36)

It seems natural, when one finds a rent in his robe of righteousness, to look for a patch. The rich young ruler came looking for just one more patch, and Jesus showed him that his whole garment was worn out. Nicodemus was ready to sew Jesus on as teacher, but the Master declared that he required a whole new suit. Who of us does not try to combine disparate elements in his thinking and living? We expect to serve Mammon and God, to be selfish in business and Christian in church, to drink the Lord's wine at His table and the devil's wine at the club, to kneel in the temple of Rimmon and yet maintain our little altar of Israel's soil.

O Jesus, Thou master tailor, we would discard the filthy rags of our goodness, and receive from Thee the seamless robe of true righteousness. Amen.

This one will stab deep.

> And after a while came unto him they that stood by, and said to Peter, Surely thou also art one of them; for thy speech bewrayeth thee. (Matthew 26:73)

Peter's attempt to conceal his true identity from the idlers in Caiaphas' court was a pitiful failure. His manner and his accent betrayed him. A youth leader says: "One afternoon after a strenuous hike through the woods with a group of my girl scouts, a religious emblem, which I always wear about my neck, was hanging visibly outside my uniform. One of the children, no more than eight years old, whispered to me, 'Your religion is showing.' "

Help us so to live this day, O God, that men may suspect that we have been with Jesus. Amen.

DISCOURAGEMENT AND DESPONDENCY

Do circumstances "get you down" easily?

> But none of these things move me, neither count I my life dear unto myself . . . (The Acts 20:24)

Patrice Munsel, coloratura soprano of the Metropolitan Opera Association, was badly shaken in a traffic accident in Atlanta, Georgia. She had sung in Flint, Michigan, during a raging snowstorm and left immediately by plane. The trip was so rough that she was airsick all the way. Then the cab in which she was on the way to her hotel was struck by a truck, and she suffered numerous bruises. She hastened to assure newsmen that she would not think of canceling her appearance that night. "I always feel like singing, unless I am so ill that I cannot get out of bed," she declared. A singer's career is not for weaklings. Christ expects like courage and resoluteness of those who serve Him.

❧ *Remembering Thy cross, dear Master, and Thy martyrs of old, we pray for a more serious purpose to serve Thee, in scorn of consequences. Amen.*

Build on your discouragement.

> The same followed Paul and us, and cried, saying, These men are the servants of the most high God, which shew unto us the way of salvation. (The Acts 16:17)

A monument at Enterprise, Alabama, was erected in honor of the boll weevil. The scourge of the cotton country, which many had felt would ruin the South forever, resulted in diversification and a more stable and prosperous economy. It took failure to force the farmers to a greater success. On his second missionary tour, Paul was frustrated in his plans to preach in Asia, and again in Bithynia. Discouraged, he arrived at Troas, where the vision came calling him to Macedonia, and a new world was opened to the gospel. Frequently our failures are but God's method of turning us toward more fruitful opportunities.

❧ *Father, we thank Thee for the frustrations that we can now see as blessings. Help us to discern Thy guiding hand in each day's providences. Amen.*

Have you ever realized your own worth?

> It was meet that we should make merry, and be glad: for this thy brother was dead, and is alive again, and was lost, and is found. (Luke 15:32)

In showing us the Father, Jesus also revealed to us our brothers. The love of God has as its corollary the lovableness of men. The price of redemption implies a corresponding worth in the redeemed. God so loved the world that He gave His Son to save it, so mankind must be very precious in His sight. When Jesus shows us the face of the Father, we cannot but see mirrored in that face the worth of His children. The Christian experience gives us a new vision of God, and also a no less revolutionary discovery of mankind.

Our blessed Lord, we thank Thee for teaching us to look up into the face of our Father in heaven. Enable us to see our brothers everywhere on earth. Amen.

When trouble is too great for you to cope with.

> The Lord hath chastened me sore: but he hath not given me over unto death. (Psalms 118:18)

Having failed to win the heavyweight boxing championship of the world from Max Schmeling in 1931, young Stribling was killed in a motorcycle accident. His father, who was his manager, and who idolized him, was crushed with grief. Recently he told a reporter, "After my boy died I tried liquor. It would make me forget for a little while, but then I remembered worse than ever. Then I found my way into the Church. I now read the Bible a lot, and I've learned that when trouble comes I can't cope with, I can leave it to the Lord."

We have learned, dear Father, that sorrow comes to us all. May our suffering draw us closer to Thee, the source of peace and comfort! Amen.

Who can tell the results if you remain faithful?

> Another parable put he forth unto them, saying, Thy kingdom of heaven is like to a grain of mustard seed, which a man took, and sowed in his field. (Matthew 13:31)

George Smith went to Africa as a Moravian missionary. He was there only a short time, won only one convert, a poor woman, and was driven from the country. He died shortly afterward, on his knees, praying for Africa. He seemed a failure. But a company of men stumbled onto the place where he had prayed and found a Bible he had left. Then they met the poor woman who was his convert. A hundred years later his mission counted more than thirteen thousand converts who had sprung from the ministry of George Smith.

We thank Thee, O God, that it is not left to us to make Thy kingdom grow, but that we may bring men into contact with Thee, the source of all growth. Amen.

A farmer and his powerful partner!

I can do all things through Christ which strengtheneth me. (Philippians 4:13)

A striking contrast appears between Paul's sense of weakness in his own strength, and his confidence of invincibility in Christ. So completely frustrated was he that he cried: "O wretched man that I am! who shall deliver me from the body of this death?" But having found the complete answer to his problem, he declared: "I can do all things through Christ which strengtheneth me." Explaining his unruffled calm, an old farmer said: "I have learned that the Lord won't let anything come to me that He and I together can't handle."

Teach us, O Christ, how weak we are in ourselves and how strong we may be in Thee. Amen.

The way to make your blue days bright.

My voice shalt thou hear in the morning, O Lord; in the morning will I direct my prayer unto Thee, and will look up. (Psalms 5:3)

A painting of a landscape without a touch of sky usually seems hemmed in, stifled. It needs at least a little patch of blue to release the eyes from being earth-bound. So also does the soul need an upward look every day, lest it be earth-bound, hemmed in. The Psalmist said: "In the morning will I direct my prayer unto Thee, and will look up." Man, who walks upright, is the looking-up animal. Let every day be Thanksgiving Day!

Father, we thank Thee that Thou hast spoken to us from heaven, and for the upward look that Thou hast put in our hearts. Help us to look to Thee always. Amen.

In your hands are two labels: despair and hope.

> I do set my bow in the cloud, and it shall be for a token of a covenant between me and the earth. (Genesis 9:13)

The rainbow in the clouds over a devastated earth was pointed out to Noah as the symbol of hope. A picture painted by G. F. Watts depicts a young woman seated on a globe in an attitude of despair, her eyes bandaged, and in her hands a lyre with all strings broken save one. Only one star is in the sky. Some have thought the picture should be called "Despair," but the title is "Hope." It is to show that when all else seems gone, hope endures.

We pray today, O God, for the devastated areas of the earth, that men may not lose hope, and that the floods of war come not again. Amen.

Despair only when the rebuke does not come.

> . . . My son, despise not thou the chastening of the Lord, nor faint when thou art rebuked of him. (Hebrews 12:5)

The same divine love that provides daily bread also gives fatherly discipline to God's children when it is needed. A Christian is not to take his troubles lightly, because every stroke has its lesson to teach. Neither is he to despair as though God were against him, because discipline is the act of a faithful father toward his own son. We have cause to be genuinely concerned when we are permitted to disobey God without rebuke, but we should be grateful for every stern providence that calls us back from wayward ways.

We confess, our Father, that we have been ungrateful at the time for some of Thy greatest mercies, because we recognized them not as such. Teach us to profit by Thy chastening, and to learn to thank Thee for it. Amen.

Remember that you are the astronomer.

> When I consider thy heavens, the work of thy fingers, the moon and the stars, which thou hast ordained;
> What is man. . . ? For thou hast made him a little lower than the angels, and hast crowned him with glory and honour. (Psalms 8:3, 4, 5)

Observation of the heavens impressed the writer of the Eighth Psalm with the littleness of man. It seemed to him incredible that a God who could create such a universe should even notice a race of such tiny creatures. But man's measure is not his body; it is his mind and soul. To whom could the heavens declare the glory of God except to a creature capable of thinking God's thoughts? A young scientist declared: "Astronomically speaking, man is insignificant." An older and wiser man corrected him: "Astronomically speaking, man is the astronomer."

For the gifts with which Thou hast endowed us, O God our Maker, we would glorify not ourselves, but Thee. Amen.

The encouragement of a presence!

> . . . lo, I am with you alway, even unto the end of the world. Amen. (Matthew 28:20)

The presence of the Duke of Wellington in the midst of battle is said to have given his soldiers such inspiration and strength that it was equivalent to thrusting in an entire new regiment. The promise of Jesus to be with those who make disciples for Him anywhere in the world is not merely an assurance of companionship, it is the certainty of victory. Conscious fellowship with Him on the part of each missionary means more for the success of Christian missions than all human re-enforcement.

O Thou who dost live intimately with each true missionary, draw us into fellowship in their labors. Amen.

There's no such thing as a no-talent man.

> Nay, much more those members of the body, which seem to be more feeble, are necessary. (I Corinthians 12:22)

In the parable of the talents, Jesus told of a five-talent man, a two-talent man, and a one-talent man, but not of a no-talent man, because there is no such person. Everyone has some useful ability. Paul compared the Church to a human body, in which every member is needed for a specific purpose, and all are equally honorable as part of one body. In the Church, as in the community, the most insignificant person should not feel himself unnecessary; the most prominent should not feel superior to others.

Teach us, Lord, to see the importance of the service we can render, lest we be discouraged; and the greatness of that which others do, lest we become proud. Amen.

Dare you come down from your cross?

> . . . If thou be the Son of God, come down from the cross. (Matthew 27:40)

The taunt of the tormentors, "Come down from the cross," was not new to Jesus. In the wilderness He was tempted to take an easier way. Those who would have made Him their king offered a happier alternative. In Gethsemane He faced the same choice. The suffering thief begged Him to renounce crucifixion. Who is there who bears a painful load for the sake of someone else without sometimes hearing a voice say, "If you were really strong, you would come down from that cross"? Jesus had already answered, "For this cause came I unto this hour."

Our prayer today, Christ of Calvary, is for all courageous souls who for love's sake suffer hardships. May they have fellowship with Thee. Amen.

The world cannot wait for perfect men.

> But we have this treasure in earthen vessels, that the excellency of the power may be of God, and not of us. (II Corinthians 4:7)

Many splendid people are not active in the Church because of their humility. Having high ideals for Christian workers, they feel themselves to be unworthy of doing God's work. Paul combined a deep sense of his own unworthiness with great zeal. He said: "We have this treasure in earthen vessels, that the excellency of the power may be of God, and not of us." If the Church had to wait for workers entirely worthy of their calling, her work would never be done. We, who are trying to serve, marvel constantly that God can do as good work as He does with such poor instruments.

Lord, if their guide I still must be, oh, let the little children see the teacher leaning hard on Thee. Amen.

Even though you never sway multitudes—

> Which of the prophets have not your fathers persecuted? . . . (The Acts 7:52)

A leading American recently told a group of Christian students that the great need of our times was for a Paul or an Isaiah to arise, to call the people back to the ways of righteousness.

"Who knows," he added, "but that such a one may be among this group?" But prophets have not been popular. Isaiah was called to preach to a diminishing congregation. Paul, near death, wrote: "Only Luke is with me." John the Baptist died in a dungeon, and Jesus was undefended before Pilate. "To dungeon, axe, and stake succeed heirs of the old heroic strain." They did not sway multitudes, but they spoke eternal truth, and revealed a way still open to those who will walk in it.

❧ *God of the prophets and martyrs, forgive us if we have waited for a voice that would make righteousness popular. Teach us the ways that are eternally right. Amen.*

For you who think your burden is heavy:

For my yoke is easy, and my burden is light. (Matthew 11:30)

A teacher in a mission school read the text, "My yoke is easy." Turning to the children, she asked, "Who can tell me what a yoke is?" A little girl of ten said, "It is something they put on the necks of animals." Then the teacher inquired, "And what is the meaning of God's yoke?" All were silent for the moment. Then the hand of a little four-year-old went up, and she said, "It is God putting His arms around our necks."

❧ *Every burden that we have to bear for Thee, blessed Lord, speaks to us of thy love and confidence in us. May our love for Thee keep us faithful. Amen.*

The disappointments of answered prayers:

For every one that asketh receiveth; and he that seeketh findeth; and to him that knocketh it shall be opened. (Luke 11:10)

Jesus did not say: "Ask and ye shall receive exactly the thing asked in exactly the way you conceive it." He did say: "Ask, and ye shall receive." Frequently the thing received is far better than that which was asked. We come, asking the things we want. We are led to seek the thing we need, and we knock for access to the presence of God. There we find what is the good, ask only for it, and receive it.

❧ *Lord, teach us to pray, not only that we may get what we want, but that we may want what Thou seest that we need. Amen.*

Are you acting as if God were dead?

> And let the peace of God rule in your hearts, to the which also ye are called in one body; and be ye thankful. (Colossians 3:15)

Martin Luther tells how he became despondent and hopeless because of his own sinfulness, the wickedness of the world, and the dangers that beset the Church. One day his wife appeared, dressed in black, and when asked the reason, replied: "Do you not know? God is dead." In astonishment he replied: "What nonsense! How can God die? He is immortal and will live through all eternity." "And yet," she said quietly, "you go about hopeless and discouraged." "Then I observed," says Luther, "what a wise woman my wife was, and mastered my silence."

O God, our help in ages past, our hope for years to come, be Thou our guide while life shall last, and our eternal home. Amen.

Try singing away the rough places of life.

> And he hath put a new song in my mouth, even praise unto our God: many shall see it, and fear, and shall trust in the Lord. (Psalms 40:3)

Recently I heard a man who grew up amid the rigors of pioneer life telling of the hardships endured by his mother. She reared a family of seven children, not only doing her own housework, but laboring in the fields and cutting firewood in the forests. Her husband, an austere and thrifty man, worked hard with her, but was unsympathetic with her religious devotion and efforts to give Christian training to the children. "She was the greatest Christian I ever knew," declared a son. "She was a singing Christian. As she worked, she sang the great old hymns. I think she was able to live as she did because of the kind of music that was in her soul."

We thank Thee, Lord, for a faith that makes us sing and for the hymns that express our devotion. Amen.

Even burdens may become bridges.

> . . . and on him they laid the cross, that he might bear it after Jesus. (Luke 23:26)

Simon of Cyrene is immortal because he carried Christ's cross.

He would never have reached Calvary, the highest mountain in history, except by cross-bearing. A biologist tells how he watched an ant carrying a piece of straw which seemed a burden to it. The ant came to a crack in the ground which was too big for it to cross. It stood for a time, as though pondering the situation, then put the straw across the crack and walked over upon it. The burden became the bridge for progress. No man can fulfill his destiny or reach real heights without carrying loads.

O Thou who didst bear a cross for us, we thank Thee for those which we carry in our hearts. We ask not for lighter burdens, but for strength to carry greater ones in Thy spirit. Amen.

Are you looking for a way out or a way in?

For I am in a strait betwixt two, having a desire to depart, and to be with Christ; which is far better. (Philippians 1:23)

A young woman said to me recently, "You will think I'm awful when I tell you that I have wished I could die." Her confession was not as shocking as she had thought it would be. The apostle Paul wrote that he had "a desire to depart, and to be with Christ; which is far better." Charles Kingsley said just before his death, "God forgive me, but I have a great curiosity to see the other world." There is this difference: my young friend was so oppressed with her present situation that she wanted to escape, while the great saints had been so impressed with the attraction of heaven that they were impatient to arrive there.

Father, in whose house are many mansions, we would not hurry our going, but give us a healthy longing to be with Thee. Amen.

Have you done all you can, right where you are?

The one preach Christ of contention . . . But the other of love, knowing that I am set for the defence of the gospel. (Philippians 1:16, 17)

Asked how he could be so calm under so much pressure, Lincoln is said to have replied: "When one feels himself to be only a pipe for omnipotence to blow through, he doesn't worry much." James Russell Lowell's Kossuth says: "I was the chosen trump through whom Our God sent forth awakening breath." This verse is made clearer in the revised version: "I am put here for the defence of the gospel." The picture is of God picking Paul up bodily in His big hand and placing him in prison, because he needed someone to speak for Him there. Passive Paul was simply an instrument for God to manipulate.

Lord of our lives, we surrender ourselves anew to Thee, asking only that Thou wilt use us as seemeth good to Thee. Amen.

Did God answer "No" when you prayed?

> And he lighted upon a certain place, and tarried there all night, because the sun was set; and he took of the stones of that place, and put them for his pillows, and lay down in that place to sleep.
> And he dreamed, and behold a ladder set up on the earth, and the top of it reached to heaven: and behold the angels of God ascending and descending on it. (Genesis 28:11, 12)

Moses, the great deliverer, was not permitted to enter the Promised Land, but he was a greater man than Joshua, who conquered Canaan. David was not permitted to build the temple of which he dreamed, but he was a nobler spirit than Solomon who did build it. Jesus prayed: "If it be possible, let this cup pass," but He is Saviour because it was not possible. Paul prayed that his thorn in the flesh might be removed, but God said: "My grace is sufficient for thee; My strength is made perfect in weakness." Some of our greatest blessings from prayer have come when God answered "No."

O wise Father, grant us the good whether we ask for it or not, and withhold from us that which is evil, though we ask for it. Amen.

A story about sand and rock.

> And the rain descended, and the floods came, and the winds blew, and beat upon that house; and it fell not: for it was founded upon a rock. . . .
> And the rain descended, and the floods came, and the winds blew, and beat upon that house; and it fell: and great was the fall of it. (Matthew 7:25, 27)

In the story of the two foundations with which Jesus concluded the Sermon on the Mount, it is significant that He twice used the same words: "And the rain descended, and the floods came, and the winds blew, and beat upon that house." Those who did the things He taught, and those who did not, apparently met the same tests. So today Christian and non-Christian alike must meet the winds of temptation, the rains of disappointment, and the floods of sorrow. Life tests every man thoroughly. The difference is that one has strength to meet it, while, like the house, another is built on sand.

Father God, we do not ask for freedom from life's storms, but for wisdom so to build that we shall not be moved by them. Amen.

Remember this when you can remember nothing else.

. . . weeping may endure for a night, but joy cometh in the morning. (Psalms 30:5)

On a sundial in Brighton, England, are these words of Richard Horne: "It is always morning somewhere in the world." It may be dark and disappointing where we are, but it will not always be so. It is always morning somewhere, and some glad, good day it will be morning everywhere. Any suffering is endurable, because it is temporary.

God of the day and the night, we thank Thee for the daily miracle of dawn, and for the assurance that all of earth's night will be followed by day. Amen.

FEAR OF TOMORROW AND DREAD OF DEATH AND OLD AGE

Suppose Columbus had been afraid of tomorrow.

> And Jesus said unto him, No man, having put his hand to the plough, and looking back, is fit for the kingdom of God: (Luke 9:62)

The courage and faith of the explorer Columbus in refusing to turn back, and pressing on to the New World are vividly described in Miller's familiar poem. Christians, too, have embarked on a great adventure. Leaving the old life, they have set forth with their faces toward a new world. As long as they keep the vision fresh, they retain the thrill of conquering explorers, but when they begin to look longingly back, their course wavers and they become unworthy of their quest.

O Thou who rulest winds and waters, help us to keep our faces set toward the city of God this day. Amen.

Age is a diploma in the school of experience.

> Thou shalt rise up before the hoary head, and honour the face of the old man, and fear thy God: I am the Lord. (Leviticus 19:32)

Ancient Judaism honored its elders. The people were expected to avoid the poor judgment that would disregard the experience of the mature, and the faulty character that would be ungrateful for services already rendered. In the early Christian Church the leaders were called "elders," suggesting that it looked for leadership to the older members. No age has seen a more virile Church.

O Thou who art the ancient of days, we thank Thee for the aged saints among us. Teach us to learn from their wisdom and to be considerate of their frailties. Amen.

Your hand on God's arm!

> For we walk by faith, not by sight. (II Corinthians 5:7)

Blind since birth, John is so familiar with the small town where he lives that he frequently goes about without a guide. It is interesting to see him counting his steps, making square turns, stopping to listen for oncoming cars. At a curb or rough place in the sidewalk he is careful, not quite sure what his foot will strike. But when his hand can rest lightly on the arm of his trusted friend, he strides along so boldly he does not seem to be blind. We all march into a future veiled by an impenetrable curtain. Guided by a trusted Friend, we walk confidently.

We have heard Thy voice saying, "Follow me," and we have placed our hand in Thine. We are grateful for the assurance with which we can now walk. Amen.

Would you want your heaven like earth?

For he looked for a city which hath foundations, whose builder and maker is God. (Hebrews 11:10)

The hope of immortality is more than mere dread of death. It is discontent with life as we have lived it and the world as we have seen it. It is faith in a God who plans something better than this. No one looks forward to another world exactly like this one, and we do not work to preserve the *status quo*. The kingdom of heaven is within us, moving us to strive for its realization here, and to hope for its perfection in the beyond.

We thank Thee, Father, that Thou hast placed eternity within our hearts. Strengthen our arms to strive for the kingdom here, and brighten our hope for its consummation in glory. Amen.

Are you giving your life for something?

. . . the Son of man came not to be ministered unto, but to minister, and to give his life a ransom for many. (Matthew 20:28)

Each of us must give his life for something. Simply clinging to life means losing it; throwing it into a great cause is saving it. Sidney Powell tells of a boy who rowed a small boat to an ice floe in a swirling, flooded river to save a rabbit he saw on it. The boat capsized and the boy drowned. The body was recovered, and a friend took the bedraggled, dead rabbit from his pocket, and said, "That's what he gave his life for!"

We offer Thee our lives, dear Saviour. Give us grace to pour them out freely in Thy service that they may be saved eternally. Amen.

Do any of the important things really change?

> Every good gift and every perfect gift is from above, and cometh down from the Father of lights . . . (James 1:17)

After many years, I visited again the spring from which as a small boy I used to drink. The appearance of the surrounding countryside was changed, but the little cove seemed strangely the same. The great oaks stand around, and the water still gurgles from between the rocks. It is not the same water that was there years ago, for the stream moves on. But the spring seems as constant as the rocks. So, I thought, God's unceasing flow of good and perfect gifts moves on. Today's blessings are not yesterday's blessings, but they come from the same spring, and tomorrow will bring a continued flow.

Father of lights, with whom is not variableness, neither shadow of turning, we bless Thee for the unabated flow of blessings through the years. Make us as confident of Thy goodness as we are of the flow of the spring. Amen.

Discovering for yourself that your dream was true.

> Remember the days of old, consider the years of many generations: ask thy father, and he will shew thee; thy elders, and they will tell thee. (Deuteronomy 32:7)

In Jewish history young men have played a heroic part. Abraham's venture, Joseph's dreams, Moses' choice, David's daring, and Isaiah's vision all reflect honor on the spirit of youth. But each of these gave a more convincing testimony after long years of experience. Youth says: "I have seen, and so I know." Moses, the aged, in his farewell message to young Israel, said: "Ask thy father, and he will shew thee; thy elders, and they will tell thee."

God of our fathers, help us to keep the adventuring spirit of youth, while we learn the assurance that the years with Thee can bring. Amen.

Great living is "keeping on the job."

> Thy shoes shall be iron and brass; and as thy days, so shall thy strength be. (Deuteronomy 33:25)

Moses seems never to have grown old. He died on a mountaintop, looking toward unconquered fields. His blessings on the tribes of Israel breathe his pioneer spirit. Note his words to Asher: "Thy shoes shall be iron and brass; and as thy days, so shall thy strength be." To him, that was better than felt slippers and an easy chair. Great living is heavy burdens, rough roads, steep hills, with equipment and strength to conquer them.

🙶 *O Thou great God, who art revealed to us in a man climbing a hill with a cross, forgive our love of ease, which is friendship with death, and give us courage and strength to live. Amen.*

There's sugar at the bottom of the cup.

They shall still bring forth fruit in old age; they shall be fat and flourishing. (Psalms 92:14)

Childhood is the happiest time of life, we have always been told. Everyone knows this except children. Older people have forgotten the acuteness of pain, the difficulty of making adjustments, and all the fear and uncertainty. A wise woman who was growing old happily once said: "All of the sugar is at the bottom of the cup." Of course the body is aging and deteriorating, and its satisfactions become less. But spiritual joys, for those who have learned to live, may be increasing. Age has profound lessons to teach and genuine joys to experience.

🙶 *Our prayer for today, O Thou ancient of days, is for all of those who are going down life's westward hill, that they· may grow old gracefully and wisely. Amen.*

Which way are you looking, back or ahead?

By faith Abraham, when he was called . . . went out, not knowing whither he went. (Hebrews 11:8)

Thorwaldsen, the noted Danish sculptor, was once asked: "Which is your greatest statue?" He promptly replied: "The next one." Men of faith are always men with a forward look. Because of his faith, Abraham set his face toward the Land of Promise. Paul lived on tiptoe, reaching forth to those things which were before him. Even Jesus endured the cross because of the joy that was set before Him. Whenever a man looks back to his achievements of the past as his greatest, he is admittedly on the decline.

🙶 *God of all our tomorrows, keep our feet ever on the upward road till we shall stand before Thy throne. Amen.*

Years tell you little about a man's age.

> And it came to pass, when the time was come that he should be received up, he stedfastly set his face to go to Jerusalem. (Luke 9:51)

Youthfulness is a quality of spirit rather than a short period of life. There are men of eighty who are still planning and accomplishing thrilling things, and others in their forties who have already retired from life. When he was forty-eight, Abraham Lincoln wrote of himself as "old and withered." A few years later he was elected President of the United States, and never again referred to his age. He was too busy. A Christian ought always to look forward, for to him even death is an adventure, a tryst with his lover; and eternity is his great goal.

❧ *God of our future, give us hearts that dream and eyes that see visions of the greater things that lie out before us. We ask it in Jesus' name. Amen.*

The trail has been blazed before you.

> . . . I also suffer these things: nevertheless I am not ashamed: for I know whom I have believed . . . (II Timothy 1:12)

Sir Michael Faraday, the great scientist who was also a great Christian, when he was on his death bed was questioned by some journalists as to his speculations concerning the soul and death. "Speculations?" said the dying man in astonishment, "I know nothing about speculations; I'm resting on certainties!" Then he quoted: "I know whom I have believed, and am persuaded that He is able to keep that which I have committed unto Him against that day."

❧ *In a world of so many uncertainties we are grateful for Thee, O Lord our rock. On Thee we rest without a doubt or fear. Amen.*

Are you homesick for the comfortable past?

> And truly, if they had been mindful of that country from whence they came out, they might have had opportunity to have returned. (Hebrews 11:15)

From wicked Sodom, Lot's wife followed her husband reluctantly, looking back fondly toward the city whose way of life she loved. Because her heart had not left it, she shared its destruction. Many hearers of Jesus were attracted to become His followers, but were loath to break with the old life. They said: "Let me have a farewell party!" "Let me have a funeral!" But Jesus said: "No man, having put his hand to the plough, and looking back, is fit for the kingdom of God."

We confess, dear Saviour, that even after knowing freedom, we sometimes long for our old chains. Help us to keep our faces forward toward our redemption. Amen.

Unknown dragons are always the biggest.

Whereas ye know not what shall be on the morrow. For what is your life? It is even a vapour, that appeareth for a little time, and then vanisheth away. (James 4:14)

Mariners' charts in the fifteenth century outlined rather crudely the shoreline of Europe and Africa, but out in the Atlantic, beyond the place where ships had ventured, were legends: "Here be dragons," and "Here be demons that devour men." Being unknown, that territory was dreadful. Every living person is proceeding constantly into unexplored territory. No one has ever ventured into tomorrow, but we must go into it. Our light is not bright enough to see what it will bring, but our faith is sufficient to go on unafraid, with Christ as guide.

Guide us, O Lord, through this and every day. For Thy sake. Amen.

We are never old until we are afraid.

. . . and now, lo, I am this day fourscore and five years old. As yet I am as strong this day as I was in the day that Moses sent me . . . Now therefore give me this mountain . . . if so be the Lord will be with me, then I shall be able to drive them out . . . (Joshua 14:10-12)

Caleb belonged to the gallant fellowship of those who refuse to grow old. At eighty-five he might have asked for security and a pension, instead he asked for a hard and hazardous reward: the right to take possession of the mountain where the giants lived. We never grow senile seeking opportunities to serve and while our faces are toward the future.

O Thou ageless God, keep alive in our breasts the youthful spirit of adventure, optimism, and self-sacrifice. We ask it in Jesus' name. Amen.

Build your canoe for the broad ocean.

> In my Father's house are many mansions: if it were not so,
> I would have told you. I go to prepare a place for you.
> (John 14:2)

Dr. J. H. Jowett, prince of preachers, now with the Lord, said: "Death is not the end; it is only a new beginning. Death is not the master of the house; he is only the porter at the king's lodge, appointed to open the gate and let the king's guests into the realm of eternal day. And so shall we ever be with the Lord. The range of our three score years and ten is not the limit of our life. Our life is not a landlocked lake enclosed within the shore lines of 70 years. It is an arm of the sea. And so we must build for those larger waters. We are immortal!"

☛ *Lord of life and eternity, we confess that there is yet a little fear of the gateway to fuller life, which we know as death. Grant us such perfect fellowship with Thee that we shall not fear anything. Amen.*

Take heart from the butterfly.

> And in nothing terrified by your adversaries: which is to
> them an evident token of perdition, but to you of salvation,
> and that of God. (Philippians 1:28)

Caterpillars were depicted in an editorial written by Arthur Brisbane as sadly carrying the corpse of a cocoon to its final resting place. The poor, distressed worms, clad in black raiment, were weeping, and all the while the beautiful butterfly fluttered happily above the muck and mire of earth, forever freed from its earthly shell. So foolish are we who, when our loved ones pass, concentrate our attention on the cocoon— the remains—while forgetting the bright butterfly.

☛ *Open the eyes of Thy bereaved children, Father, that they may see their lost loved ones not as dead, but as alive for evermore. Amen.*

SORROW AND BEREAVEMENT

When life tumbles in.

> Let Israel hope in the Lord: for with the Lord there is mercy, and with him is plenteous redemption. (Psalms 130:7)

A Christian has no better opportunity to demonstrate the power of Christ in his life than by the way he bears sorrow. One of Scotland's most effective preachers is Arthur John Gossip of Glasgow. One day his wife suddenly died, and his life was plunged into gloom. It was expected that he would not be in his pulpit the following Sunday. Thinking of running away, he said to himself: "No, I will not deny her for anything." He preached a sermon that has become famous: "When Life Tumbles In." Life had tumbled in, but he caught his hearers up within the lifting sweep of his own great faith, which had been made doubly sure through the deeper insights that had come to him in his great personal loss.

❧ We pray that grace may be given us, Lord, not only to make our troubles work together for our good, but that they may be used to bless others. Amen.

Tomorrow your eyes will be clearer.

> And I will give her her vineyards from thence, and the valley of Achor for a door of hope: and she shall sing there, as in the days of her youth . . . (Hosea 2:15)

The valley of Achor received its name from the terrible death there of Achan and his family, because of his sin. It means "valley of trouble." Prophesying that Israel's dark night will bring a new dawn, Hosea says: "I will give her . . . the valley of Achor for a door of hope." Huntington says beautifully: "Sorrow is our John the Baptist, clad in grim garments, with rough arms, a son of the wilderness, baptizing us with bitter tears, preaching repentance; and behind him comes the gracious, affectionate, healing Lord, speaking peace and joy to the soul."

❧ O Thou man of sorrows, we thank Thee for eyes that see clearer because they have been washed with tears, and hearts that are more tender for having been broken. Amen.

Sorrow gives you new kinship with others.

> For as the sufferings of Christ abound in us, so our consolation also aboundeth by Christ. (II Corinthians 1:5)

Misery, we are told, loves company. Certainly those who suffer find solace in the fellowship of others who have had similar experiences. One who is passing through sorrow now wrote to a friend who is in the same trouble: "I feel that we are walking this way together. Although we are far apart, it seems that I can reach out in the dark and touch your bowed shoulder." The New Testament Christians felt that Christ could better comfort His troubled followers because He had suffered. In our darkness, we can reach out and touch Him. His shoulder is bowed under a cross, and His hands are torn.

Blessed Saviour, may everything we suffer bring us into closer fellowship with Thee. Amen.

Your sorrow lifts you to a new sympathy for others.

> Remember them that are in bonds, as bound with them; and them which suffer adversity, as being yourselves also in the body. (Hebrews 13:3)

One of the great blessings of suffering is the ability that it brings to sympathize. Our sympathy is never very deep unless founded on our own experience. We pity, but do not enter into the grief we have never felt. Our Saviour entered into our lot so completely that He weeps for our sorrows and dies for our sins. No finer statement of Christian sympathy exists anywhere than this: "Remember them that are in bonds, as bound with them; and them which suffer adversity, as being yourselves also in the body."

We thank Thee, O God, for all we have ever suffered, which taught us to share the burdens of another, in Jesus' name. Amen.

When Easter comes to your own household.

> When Jesus therefore saw her weeping, and the Jews also weeping which came with her, he groaned in the spirit, and was troubled. (John 11:33)

Sweethearts after almost thirty years of married life, Jane and John were completely devoted to each other, and both were radiant Christians. On Easter morning John suffered a heart attack, and almost in an instant he was gone. When the pastor arrived, Jane's face was almost glowing. "For him it is the loveliest Easter ever," she said. "For a week I have been studying the resurrection story to teach my Sunday-school class. And now John and I are living it."

Lord of life, who hast said, "He that liveth and believeth in me shall never die," we pray for all of Thy bereaved children that they may rejoice in hope. Amen.

Where does the sweetest music come from?

But none saith, Where is God my maker, who giveth songs in the night . . . (Job 35:10)

The audience listened appreciatively as Marian Anderson sang a program of Norwegian compositions beautifully. But when, as an encore, she began to sing a familiar American Negro spiritual, they could hardly restrain their applause until she finished, and then it lasted in waves for minutes. Why do these spirituals move us so much? Is it not through the undertone of suffering from the heart of an oppressed people? They are songs given in the night. The sweetest music always comes out of sadness.

God of sorrowing Israel and of all Thy suffering children, we thank Thee for the dark nights in which Thou hast walked with Thy children and taught them to sing. Amen.

Do you dread what you are afraid may happen?

But now he is dead, wherefore should I fast? can I bring him back again? I shall go to him, but he shall not return to me. (II Samuel 12:23)

During the illness of his infant son, David fasted and prayed in agony. When the child died, the servants feared to tell him lest his grief should pass all bounds. Instead, when he learned that death had come, he arose, bathed, ate food, and reasserted his faith in God and immortality. Many of us have walked that path. While uncertainty remains, we agonize. But when sorrow's finality comes, God gives peace that passeth understanding.

God of all comfort, we thank Thee for grace sufficient in sorrow. We pray for every broken heart in the world to know that grace. Amen.

Do you know where the rock foundations are?

> It is good for me that I have been afflicted; that I might
> learn thy statutes. (Psalms 119:71)

"Tears," said Henry Ward Beecher, "are often the telescope through which men see far into heaven." Many of us can say with the ancient writer of songs: "Before I was afflicted, I went astray." And then we add sincerely: "It is good for me that I have been afflicted." There are spiritual giants among us who can date their real beginnings of spiritual growth from some great sorrow. It takes floods and winds to show some of us where rock foundations are. God's children have found that the clearest light by which to see the Son of Man is the light of the fiery furnace.

Dear God of comfort, we do not pray for sorrow to come, but we ask that Thou wilt lead us to receive all the blessings hidden in the sorrow Thou dost send. Amen.

In prison he talked about happiness.

> Acquaint now thyself with him, and be at peace: thereby
> good shall come unto thee. (Job 22:21)

One almost cringes at Paul's review of what he had suffered for Christ, in beatings, in stonings, shipwreck, imprisonment, sickness, pain, cold, nakedness, deprivation, and every kind of danger. Yet he spoke of peace more frequently than all other New Testament writers combined. Always for him the source of peace was God, and the presence of God in the heart guaranteed peace. Though in prison, he wrote: "The peace of God, which passeth all understanding, shall keep your hearts and minds through Christ Jesus."

We have prayed, Father, and we pray again, for peace in the world, but give us in our hearts Thy peace, which does not depend on the world. We ask it in Jesus' name. Amen.

Sorrow is always in the present tense.

> With the ancient is wisdom; and in length of days under-
> standing. (Job 12:12)

Time is our friend. It is the great teacher, and wisdom is not gained without it. It is the kind healer of wounds. Daily in the hospital I see patients in pain who tomorrow will be more comfortable. "Time," said Benjamin Disraeli, "is a great physician." Even the pain of a broken heart, that today seems unbearable, will be assuaged by the tender hand of time, our foster nurse when sorrows come. It gives us room to work, and sometimes of itself solves our problem.

❦ O Thou ancient of days, we thank Thee for this day, with the recognized blessings it brings, and all that we receive unconsciously from it. Amen.

How to regain your equilibrium after bereavement.

> Simon Peter saith unto them, I go a fishing. They say unto him, We also go with thee. They went forth, and entered into a ship immediately; and that night they caught nothing. (John 21:3)

Simon Peter was a fisherman. For years his hands had been accustomed to handling wet nets and his cheeks to feeling cold spray. After his Master's death, when sorrow, loneliness, and regret became unbearable, he turned back to his old mechanical toil. A wise instinct guided him. When numbing sorrow strikes, one is usually helpless for a little while, and then one may discover that familiar toil with the hands is the most effective anesthetic for an aching heart. After a night of dogged labor, the Master comes, and it is dawn.

❦ The gift of work has blessed us, Master, not only in worth-while accomplishment, but also in the therapy of our souls. We thank Thee. Amen.

Would you actually part with your sorrows?

> . . . but we glory in tribulations also: knowing that tribulation worketh patience. (Romans 5:3)

A mother who recently lost a lovely baby daughter writes: "It hurts almost unbearably, but nobody can ever take from us those two years she was with us. If sorrow is a part of keeping those precious memories, I don't want ever to lose my sorrow." She is not clinging morbidly to her grief, but simply feels that her life has been enriched. Few of us would be willing to surrender our sorrows with all that is related to them.

❦ O Thou man of sorrows and acquainted with grief, teach us to have fellowship with Thee in our sufferings, and to know Thy tender nearness. Amen.

Perhaps your own burden fits you best.

> Giving thanks always for all things unto God . . . (Ephesians 5:20)

An old legend tells that all the people were invited to lay their burdens in one great heap. Then each had the privilege of selecting the one which he preferred. After a good deal of examination and thought, each selected the burden he had laid down. Our burdens are inextricably linked with our loved ones, friends, and joys. If we knew all about both, most of us would prefer our own lives to any other.

🙚 *Good Father, we often complain, but we would not exchange our lot for any other. Forgive our ingratitude, and give us joy in our blessings. Amen.*

The Shepherd in the valley of the shadow.

> He maketh me to lie down in green pastures: he leadeth me beside the still waters. . . .
> Yea, though I walk through the valley of the shadow of death, I will fear no evil: for thou art with me; thy rod and thy staff they comfort me. (Psalms 23:2, 4)

The contrast between the second and fourth verses of the Twenty-Third Psalm emphasizes an important fact about religious experience. When we walk in green pastures and beside still waters, it is not hard to believe that the Shepherd is leading us. But the way home lies through dark chasms, where the shadows are heavy. God is our guide there, too, and is often more real to us than in the sunlight. We learn to fear no evil, not because evil does not exist, but because His rod and staff protect and support us.

🙚 *O Thou good shepherd of our souls, we thank Thee for the green pastures and still waters of life, and we are no less grateful for Thy guiding presence in the dark shadow days. Amen.*

The visions that come in deep valleys.

> The burden of the valley of vision. What aileth thee now, that thou art wholly gone up to the house tops? (Isaiah 22:1)

Mountaintops are the places from which one expects to see landscapes and heavenly things. Why, then, does Isaiah speak

of the "valley of vision"? It seems strange. Yet is it not true
that our most significant visions have come when we were
brought low? We have seen God and the things He would
show us most clearly when we walked through dark valleys.

*O Thou who didst make our eyes and our hearts, teach
us to see the things that can be discerned only from the
vantage point of the deep valley. Amen.*

That man you passed, he has a heartache, too.

> But when he saw the multitudes, he was moved with com-
> passion on them, because they fainted, and were scattered
> abroad . . . (Matthew 9:36)

A pastor who lives long with one church and enjoys the confidence of the people, learns much about them. One definite
conviction he reaches is that there are no human beings without problems and very few without heartaches. Yet so cleverly
do they hide their worries from each other that every person
feels that he alone is burdened. If, as we walk down the street,
we could only know how weak each person feels, how unworthy, and how many fears haunt him, I rather think our
hearts would go out in sympathy to every person we meet.

*Father, make us conscious of the weakness of others, that
we may be compassionate; and of our own weakness, that we
be not condescending. Amen.*

INJUSTICES IN LIFE—LACK OF STANDARDS AND VALUES IN OTHERS

Will you join the parade, or lead it?

> I pray not that thou shouldest take them out of the world, but that thou shouldest keep them from the evil. (John 17:15)

If everyone else would live by the Sermon on the Mount, how easy it would be to join the others. But we do not have a Christian world, nor even a Christian America. The godly society is yet to be created. Admittedly, it is difficult to live a Christian life in a pagan world. But that is the only kind of Christian one can be. If the gospel of Christ cannot meet that test, it is of no use in our kind of world. The Christian is to be in the world but not of it. It does not own him. Though outnumbering him many times over, it cannot vote him down.

Dear Father of the faithful, we pray not that Thou wilt take us out of the world, but that Thou wilt keep us from the evil one. For Jesus' sake. Amen.

Do you practice the "balcony philosophy"?

> And now I say unto you, Refrain from these men, and let them alone: for if this counsel or this work be of men, it will come to nought:
> But if it be of God, ye cannot overthrow it; lest haply ye be found even to fight against God. (The Acts 5:38, 39)

"Let them alone: for if this . . . be of men, it will come to nought: But if it be of God, ye cannot overthrow it." Gamaliel had what Dr. John Mackay calls the "balcony philosophy." He would sit on the sideline and watch the struggle. In the face of wrong, duty does not sit apathetically waiting for God to destroy it. We must be His instruments in opposing it. In the cause of right, we are not called to be curious spectators, watching to see what God will do. Rather we must throw all our strength on God's side. Lowell was right: "They are slaves who dare not be in the right with two or three."

Our Sovereign Lord, save us from the spirit of Gamaliel, who said, "Let them alone," and fill us with the spirit of the apostles who said, "We must obey God." Amen.

Suppose someone hurts you unjustly.

> . . . it was not you that sent me hither, but God: and he
> hath made me a father to Pharaoh, and lord of all his house,
> and a ruler throughout all the land of Egypt. (Genesis 45:8)

Joseph's jealous brothers sold him to slave traders, and God
used their crime to make him a great man. Moses murdered
an Egyptian, but by his act he was driven into the desert for
preparation to be Israel's deliverer. Pharaoh's cruelty was used
to move the Hebrews toward their high destiny. By the crime
of the crucifiers a Redeemer was provided for the world. Persecution of the Church became the wind that spread the sparks
of the gospel. Always when the adversary has raised his sword
against the Lord's anointed, an unseen hand has deflected the
blow and used its force to clear a new path.

*O God of providence, give us faith to believe that Thou
art working out Thy purpose, even in the things that men
mean for evil. We ask it in Jesus' name. Amen.*

Has an unjust blow upon another hurt you?

> . . . Inasmuch as ye have done it unto one of the least of
> these my brethren, ye have done it unto me. (Matthew
> 25:40)

Jesus said: "Inasmuch as ye have done it unto one of the least
of these my brethren, ye have done it unto me." If, then, He
feels the force of every blow aimed at one of His own, surely
the marks of Calvary must be hidden under fresh wounds.
Can we see on His body the welt raised by the masked hood-
lum's lash, the bayonet wounds, the gauntness of hunger about
which we have not cared?

*Tenderhearted Saviour, teach us what it means to suffer
with all who are in pain. Give us a heart like Thine. Amen.*

Many axioms that will stand challenging.

> Ye have heard that it hath been said, Thou shalt love thy
> neighbour, and hate thine enemy. (Matthew 5:43)

Asked how he came to discover relativity, Albert Einstein is
said to have replied: "I challenged an axiom." That is what
Jesus did: "Ye have heard . . . But I say unto you . . ."
"An eye for an eye, and a tooth for a tooth." That was axio-
matic, but He challenged it: "Resist not evil." "Love thy

neighbour, and hate thine enemy." Of course! But he objected: "Love your enemies." We have our axioms: "When in Rome, do as the Romans do." "My country, right or wrong." "A man must live." How many of our axioms ought to be challenged?

Save us, O God, from the error of making triteness the test of truth. Amen.

What about the sins of respectable people?

> But Jesus perceived their wickedness, and said, Why tempt ye me, ye hypocrites? (Matthew 22:18)

A hypocrite, originally, was an actor who wore a mask to portray a part on a stage. The people whom Jesus called hypocrites were not masked villains nor deliberate deceivers, but religious, decent, and respected people, who behind an impressive façade were self-righteous, self-centered, and self-seeking. The greatest sin is a stubborn determination to remain master and sovereign of one's own soul, rejecting God's claim to dominion. That sin parades as virtue. The great sins that blight the world are committed by respectable people. Trusted and honored community leaders crucified Jesus.

O Thou convicting spirit, give us to see ourselves behind our masks of self-righteousness, in desperate need of redemption. Amen.

Do the forces of wrong seem to be winning?

> For he must reign, till he hath put all enemies under his feet. (I Corinthians 15:25)

The Roman roads were built by Caesar to subjugate conquered peoples. Paul and others used them to carry the gospel throughout the Empire. The tyrant fell; the gospel marches on. The powerful enemies of Jesus won their victory; they crucified Him. But the cross on which they thought to put an end to Him forever became a magnet to draw all men to Him. D. R. Davies says: "At any one moment, sin is stronger, but in the total process, it is always weaker; for it is self-destructive."

Holy Father, whose very being guarantees the ultimate victory of truth and righteousness, we trust Thee and dedicate ourselves to Thy will. Amen.

The right to make a living.

> No man shall take the nether or the upper millstone to pledge: for he taketh a man's life to pledge. (Deuteronomy 24:6)

Moses would not permit a man to be deprived of that from which he earned a living, though other possessions might be taken from him. Job security was considered more vital than the safety of property. Those nations that have put property rights above human rights have discovered to their sorrow that the property has been lost. No one can guarantee that any man will work, and it is difficult to devise a system by which all will be guaranteed the privilege of working. But it is the right of every man and must somehow be secured.

Father, we thank Thee for the privilege of earning our daily bread. We pray that every man in the world may have and prize that blessing. Amen.

"As common as a cold" is not a good apology.

> For many are called, but few are chosen. (Matthew 22:14)

A well-known writer has said: "Sins do not become virtues by being widely practiced. Right is still right if nobody is right, and wrong is wrong if everybody is wrong. Some have contended that sex aberrations are as common as the common cold, but nobody has so far asked us to consider them normal and desirable." Jesus warned that the right road would not be popular, and the popular road would not be right.

Save us, Lord, from the dangerous sense of security in numbers, and give us courage to walk alone, if need be, in the right. Amen.

An evil calls forth a deliverer. You may be he.

> And I will make of thee a great nation, and I will bless thee, and make thy name great; and thou shalt be a blessing. (Genesis 12:2)

Dr. Clarence Macartney has observed that great men are to a certain extent the product of their day and generation. At any other period of America's history than the Revolution, George Washington might have been just a well-to-do Virginia planter. Except for the dispute over slavery and union, Lincoln might have been an obscure country lawyer. So with the great men of the Bible. Moses came when Israel needed a deliverer. Gideon arose when Midian oppressed Israel. Any man is great who is used of God for a needed service in our own day.

❧ *O Thou who dost work out Thy purposes in human lives, we pray not for fame or power, but for vision to see where Thou dost need us. Amen.*

You can be a kindler.

> . . . God hath chosen the foolish things of the world to confound the wise; and God hath chosen the weak things of the world to confound the things which are mighty. (I Corinthians 1:27)

The sneer that Providence is always on the side of the biggest battalions is an audacious misreading of history. The greatest battles of history have all been won by slender forces. Every good cause first kindled a flame in the hearts of a few nobodies, whom the world either killed or laughed to scorn. But the convictions grew until one day the world waked up to find that everybody believed them. Eleven obscure men against the world made a weak battalion, but they were on God's side, and that made the difference.

❧ *O Thou who art with two or three who stand in Thy name, help us to be less concerned about the number of our allies, and more concerned for the justice of our cause. Amen.*

A word about your next Congressman.

> Hate the evil, and love the good, and establish judgment in the gate . . . (Amos 5:15)

The preacher of righteousness, Amos, was concerned about corruption in the political life of Israel, and he appealed for the right kind of citizenship. The first requirement concerned personal character: "Hate the evil, and love the good." Only a good man can be a good citizen. He must oppose evil, not only officially, but privately. He must embrace the good, not only in public, but in his heart. Then Amos adds the essential requirement for public affairs: "Establish judgment in the gate."

❧ *God of our fathers, we thank Thee for the freedom we enjoy. Teach us to know and do our duty as citizens. Amen.*

Can you endure without surrendering?

> Strengthened with all might, according to his glorious power, unto all patience and longsuffering with joyfulness. (Colossians 1:11)

The great test of spiritual strength is not activity, but the practice of passive virtues: "Strengthened . . . unto all patience and longsuffering with joyfulness." Patience is the opposite of cowardice or despondency. Longsuffering is in contrast with wrath and revenge. The sinewy character is the one that can endure sorrow, loss, and disappointment without surrendering to despondency. He is truly strong who can face injustices, unfair criticism, and persecution without anger or a vengeful spirit. Both endurance and action are needed in life, but endurance is the harder to build.

Dear Father, teach us to be patient as Jesus was under life's burdens and tests. We ask it in His name. Amen.

Why does God permit so many injustices?

> The Lord is not slack concerning his promise . . . but is longsuffering . . . not willing that any should perish, but that all should come to repentance. (II Peter 3:9)

Can God be righteous and yet permit so much wickedness in His world? Paul answers: "Yes; it is because He is good that He is so patient with men. His saving me shows how longsuffering He is." Peter adds: "The Lord is not slack concerning His promise . . . but is longsuffering . . . not willing that any should perish, but that all should come to repentance."

We thank Thee, righteous Father, that Thou hast been patient with sinful men. May Thy longsuffering not make us presumptuous, but lead us to repentance. Amen.

This is our nation's weakest link.

> Righteousness exalteth a nation: but sin is a reproach to any people. (Proverbs 14:34)

The great wall of China is one of the wonders of the world. Twenty feet high, thirteen feet wide at the top, with towers for garrisons about every hundred yards, it extends over mountains and plains for fourteen hundred miles. It was built about 210 B.C. to prevent invasion by the barbarians from the north. But because of a fatal weakness, it was breached a number of times during the first few years after it was built. How? The guards were bribed. No nation can be stronger than the character of its people.

❧ We pray for our nation to be strong, O God, not merely in flimsy armaments, but in the integrity of its people. Amen.

Your candle can better be seen in the darkness.

Jesus answered . . . Except a man be born again, he cannot see the kingdom of God. (John 3:3)

In the muck and slime of a stagnant pond, a water lily blooms in spotless purity. It seems more breathlessly beautiful because of the contrast with its environment, and at the same time the whole pond is transformed into a mirrored setting for the one perfect flower. So Christian character is made evident by contrast with un-Christian surroundings, and a sordid society is changed as it becomes the setting for a beautiful life. The Hebrew children did a better job of godly living in the fiery furnace than did Adam and Eve in the garden of Eden.

❧ Father, we pray that in our dark world we may find, not an excuse for dullness, but an occasion to shine. Amen.

How may we have a warless world?

Then judgment shall dwell in the wilderness, and righteousness remain in the fruitful field.
And the work of righteousness shall be peace and the effect of righteousness quietness and assurance for ever. (Isaiah 32:16, 17)

In his vision of a future era of peace, Isaiah saw that certain conditions were necessary for it. It would be sent from God, when the spirit should be poured upon us from on high. It would be accompanied with material blessings, for the wilderness would be a fruitful field—starving people do not enjoy peace. And it would result from moral and spiritual preparation.

❧ O Thou who art the prince of peace, teach us not only to long for a warless world, but to pray and strive for a righteous world. Amen.

INFLUENCES OF THE PAST

You owe your parents more than you think.

> Honour thy father and thy mother: that thy days may be long . . . (Exodus 20:12)

The Fifth Commandment bids us honor our fathers and mothers, not boast of them. It is observed by obedience to our parents in our youth and kindness and consideration for them as age advances. We are the products of their training, and they are most honored by our living good and useful lives.

Heavenly Father, we thank Thee for our earthly parents who have bequeathed to us an honorable name and a goodly heritage. May our lives honor them, and may our children receive no less from us! Amen.

Suppose, somewhere, the light had gone out.

> Ye are the light of the world. A city that is set on an hill cannot be hid. (Matthew 5:14)

All the congregation sat in darkness, while one match was struck and a tiny candle lighted. Another candle, touched to the lighted one, sprang into flame. It, in turn, touched another, and so the light spread, driving back the darkness until the whole house was lighted. So Jesus, the light of the world, drew a small group into contact with Him until they caught the flame. He told them: "Ye are the light of the world." They touched others, and so the light has spread. And everyone who has that light must pass it on.

O Thou who are the light of our lives, teach us humbly to share our light with others. For Jesus' sake. Amen.

You're standing on Thomas Edison's shoulders!

> . . . look unto the rock whence ye are hewn . . . (Isaiah 51:1)

All of us are indebted to those who have gone before us for almost everything we have. Scientific discoveries, technological progress, social gains, and political reforms worked out by them combine to give us a way of life impossible for our fathers. Similarly, we stand on the shoulders of the past for a clearer vision of God. Because of the experiences of Moses, David, Isaiah, Jesus, Paul, and all the inspired writers and leaders, we can see the face of the Father more clearly. Subsequent history has but added to their height.

God of the ages, we thank Thee for our heritage from the past, and pray that those who come after us may know Thee better because we lived. Amen.

After all, those parents have a good start on you.

> But if any widow have children or nephews, let them learn first to shew piety at home, and to requite their parents: for that is good and acceptable before God. (I Timothy 5:4)

A teacher said to a group of college girls: "You know quite a bit; but you do not intend to quit learning. You expect to know far more twenty-five years from now than you know today." They nodded approval. Then he added: "Since that is the case, it is well for you to remember that your mothers have had just about that much start on you. So you will live more wisely and probably longer if you listen to them and learn from their experience."

These lines by John S. Hoyland are our prayer: "Father, grant unto us true family love, that we may belong more entirely to those whom Thou hast given us." Amen.

And still there is much unexplored territory.

> Who is a wise man and endued with knowledge among you? let him shew out of a good conversation his works with meekness of wisdom. (James 3:13)

With keen insight, James lists meekness as a mark of the "wise man and endued with knowledge." The great scientist Isaac Newton left this comment: "I seem to have been only like a boy playing on the seashore and diverting myself in now and then finding a smoother pebble or a prettier shell than ordinary, whilst the great ocean of truth lay all undiscovered before me." We share with the wisest and most learned men who have lived the sense of reverent wonder before the marvels of God's universe.

We thank Thee, Father, for the progress made by mankind in discovering the secrets of the world Thou hast made. May we, through this knowledge, be led to worship Thee and serve Thy children. Amen.

Have you traced the thread of the past?

> O let the nations be glad and sing for joy: for thou shalt
> judge the people righteously, and govern the nations upon
> earth. (Psalms 67:4)

Canon Farrar wisely observed: "A great part of the Bible is
history, and all history rightly understood is a Bible. Its lessons
are God's methods of slowly exposing error and of guiding
into truths." Another has said: "The human story is the criticism of a loving God upon the selfish purposes of men." Since
the hand of a righteous God can be seen so clearly in history,
we may be confident that that same hand will guide the future
of our world.

꙳ *God of the nations, we are grateful for the vision of Thy
face looking at us out of the past. Give us the vision to see
Thy hinder parts marching into the future before us. Amen.*

Let the past make your mistakes for you.

> Not as though I had already attained, either were already
> perfect: but I follow after, if that I may apprehend that for
> which also I am apprehended of Christ Jesus. (Philippians
> 3:12)

A cynic has observed: "We learn from history that we don't
learn from history." Men make the same mistakes over and
over because they do not study the past. In both the Old and
New Testament the importance of the lessons of history is
stressed. The greatest fact of history is God. Remembering His
judgments, we are saved from folly; remembering His faithfulness, we are delivered from fear.

꙳ *Teach us, O God, to see Thy purposes worked out in the
record of the past, and to discover Thy will for our lives in
the present. Amen.*

Is this an age of progress?

> And Isaac digged again the wells of water, which they had
> digged in the days of Abraham his father . . . (Genesis
> 26:18)

Isaac's time was later than that of Abraham, but he found
that his people got thirsty, just as had their fathers. The wells
from which Abraham drank had been filled up by the Philis-
tines. So Isaac cleared out the rubble, that his people might
quench their thirst at the same deep springs that had sustained

those before them. Our age has been obsessed with the idea
of progress. We have so many things that are better than those
our fathers had that we assume that we are superior in all
things. But not all change is progress! Stones may be used to
build houses, but they may also be used to fill up wells. There
are wells from which our fathers drank, and which the Philis-
tines have filled up, which sorely need to be dug again today.

*God of our fathers, help us to open again the wells of
prayer, family worship, church attendance, and Sabbath rest
that were refreshment and life to our forebears. Amen.*

Do you remember what you learned, or from whom you learned?

For I have given you an example, that ye should do as I
have done to you. (John 13:15)

Some of the skills, and only a very few of the facts, learned
in my school days have been retained. But the influence of
my teachers will be with me always. Even after more than a
score of years I find myself imitating their attitudes toward
life, their methods of approaching problems, and even their
little mannerisms. My education is, to an astonishing degree,
the aggregate of the influences of my teachers. The greatest
thing the disciples got from the teaching of Jesus was not a
doctrine, but an influence. "I have given you an example," He
told them, "that ye should do as I have done to you." Till the
last hour of their lives, the most important thing in the world
was that they had been with Him.

*O Thou great teacher, help up by daily contact to learn
of Thee, that we may teach the good way to those whose lives
we touch. Amen.*

To help you steer a true course today.

Look unto Abraham your father, and unto Sarah that bare
you . . . (Isaiah 51:2)

A humorist tells of a fabulous bird that flies backward because
he doesn't care where he's going; he just wants to see where
he's been. There are those who look toward the past for the
past's sake. But a good oarsman rows a true course forward
by looking backward intelligently. Isaiah counsels Israel:
"Look unto Abraham your father, and unto Sarah that bare
you," in order that it may go forward with confidence, "for

the Lord shall comfort Zion." The God of the past is the God of the future. The God of Valley Forge is the God of the atomic age.

O God, our help in ages past, we trust Thee as our shelter from the stormy blast, and our eternal home. Amen.

Don't discard the scrap iron.

> . . . every scribe which is instructed unto the kingdom of heaven is like unto a man that is an householder, which bringeth forth out of his treasure things new and old. (Matthew 13:52)

Uncle Gus has a little foundry where he makes a limited supply of iron castings, which are in great demand. He says his secret is to melt together in just the right proportions old scrap iron and new pig iron. The old iron contributes hardness and the new malleability. Old age and youth have each a contribution to make. The world needs the stability of mature experience and the resilience of youth.

We are glad, Father, for lives that are not static, but move on, with each successive stage important. Give us grace to live each age at its best. Amen.

CHALLENGES TO HIGHER LIVING

Respect for self is something one must earn.

Righteousness exalteth a nation . . . (Proverbs 14:34)

There is a type of love for family that expresses itself chiefly in resentment against criticism of or affronts to members of the clan. It goes "feudin' and fussin' and fightin'" on the slightest provocation. There is a finer love for family that is not concerned about defending the family honor from affronts, but is anxious that family members be worthy of respect and honor. The same distinction exists between jingoist patriotism and the love for one's country which strives to make it worthy of the respect and love of all mankind. True patriotism is not distressed about unjustified criticism, but is anxious to correct conditions that deserve criticism.

✒ *God of the nations, we thank Thee for our heritage as Americans. Help us to make ours a country that other peoples will trust and honor. Amen.*

You say: I could make a better world than this.

Ye are the salt of the earth . . . (Matthew 5:13)

As salt, Christians are in the world to save the world from rottenness. A cynic argued with an earnest Christian that the conditions in the world prove that there cannot be an intelligent and loving God. "I could make a better world than this," he declared. "Yes," replied his friend, "I think I can, too. That is why God has put me here. Let's do it." We all have the privilege of helping God make a better world.

✒ *Recognizing our rightful place as laborers together with Thee, Father, we dedicate ourselves anew to Thy world-redeeming service. Amen.*

A church for mules:

But he that lacketh these things is blind, and cannot see afar off, and hath forgotten that he was purged from his old sins. (II Peter 1:9)

A stranger passing some mines in Pennsylvania many years ago asked a little boy why a field was so full of mules. "These mules are workers in the mines during the week," replied the boy, "and are brought up into the sunlight on Sunday to keep them from going blind." Regular worship brings the soul into God's sunlight and keeps spiritual vision clear.

Meet with us today as we worship Thee, O Christ, and heal our spiritual blindness. Amen.

A challenge to make the heart beat fast.

. . . I came not to send peace, but a sword. (Matthew 10:34)

Christ attracted His disciples, not with word pictures of the delights of heaven, but with a challenge to throw their lives into a cause, His kingdom. Garibaldi of Italy challenged his soldiers: "What I have to offer you is fatigue, danger, struggle and death; the chill of the cold night in the free air, and heat under the burning sun; no lodgings, no munitions, no provisions, but forced marches, dangerous watchposts, and the continual struggle with the bayonet against batteries; those who love freedom and their country may follow me."

Confessing that we have been concerned for a comfortable Christianity for ourselves, we pray for more of the spirit that is ready to die to give Christian comfort to a broken world. Amen.

Does anyone ever come to you for help?

. . . for this cause I obtained mercy, that in me first Jesus Christ might shew forth all longsuffering, for a pattern to them which should hereafter believe on him to life everlasting. (I Timothy 1:16)

One who has traveled in Asia Minor reports that the women there may be seen each day at dawn going outdoors and looking at the chimneys of their neighbors. Discovering one out of which smoke is coming, they go to that house to borrow live coals with which to kindle fires in their own homes. Only those who have a living fire can share it. So people who seek spiritual warmth must go to those whose lives give evidence of the presence of a spiritual flame.

Father God, in a world in which so many hearts are painfully cold, we thank Thee for those whose hearts are warm with Thy love. Amen.

Which end of religion are you looking at?

> There is a river, the streams whereof shall make glad the city of God, the holy place of the tabernacles of the Most High. (Psalms 46:4)

A cynical young man once said to Dr. Henry Sloane Coffin, "Well, what is there to religion, anyway?" Dr. Coffin pointed out the window. "What is there to the Hudson River? Away yonder in the Adirondacks near its source, it is only a little brook, It flows on until it becomes a stream, along whose banks hundreds of summer campers find rest and renewal. It flows on until it becomes a river, furnishing water and power and light to whole cities. It flows on until it reaches its mouth, where it sweeps away the sewage of our greatest city out into the ocean depths."

We thank Thee, O God, for what true religion means to our thirsty, tired, and soiled race. We pray that every life may be blessed by it. Amen.

Here you may breathe the air of eternity!

> Thy word is a lamp unto my feet, and a light unto my path. (Psalms 119:105)

Daily guidance from Bible reading does not require that we find, though we sometimes do, a passage that deals explicitly with our immediate problem. The whole Word breathes the air of eternity. As we read we are lifted up to God's point of view, and so see our lives in a different perspective. Against the background of eternal truth, things are seen as they are. Frequently our difficulty is not that we are not wise enough to solve our problems, but that we have lost our perspective.

We have found, O God, that Thy Word is a lamp to our feet and a light to our path.. Forgive us that we sometimes stumble along in darkness because we will not use the light. Amen.

Perhaps you'll be the one who'll try it.

> Then said Jesus to them again, Peace be unto you: as my Father hath sent me, even so send I you. (John 20:21)

Marco Polo, returning from a tour of China, is said to have brought word that Kublai Khan had besought him to send back a hundred intelligent Christians who could explain their faith, defend it against all assaults, and live it before the Chinese in quiet, eloquent testimony. After a great deal of difficulty, two men were found who would go, but after proceeding part of the way, they became fearful and turned back. "Christianity," said a critic, "has been tried and found wanting." "No," sadly replied another, "it has been found difficult, and not tried."

Forgive, O Lord, our shabby interpretation of Thy life, and lead us so to live that the world may see Thy likeness in us. Amen.

What you see will make you what you become.

For to me to live is Christ, and to die is gain. (Philippians 1:21)

When he was nine years old Bobby Feller, star pitcher for the Cleveland Indians, the 1948 World Series champions, was asked by his teacher to write a theme about a great oak tree. He wrote about how it could be cut down and made into baseball bats and home plates. Even in childhood he could say, "To me to live is baseball." There are those who can say, "To me to live is money." Others, "To me to live is pleasure." Paul declared, "To me to live is Christ."

Lord Jesus, who dost gather in Thyself all of life's lasting values, we dedicate ourselves to Thee. Give us the joy of being useful to Thee. Amen.

On what kind of timetable are you running?

If we confess our sins, he is faithful and just to forgive us our sins, and to cleanse us from all unrighteousness. (I John 1:9)

The goal of Christian living is to be like Christ, in His crystal purity, His utter devotion to the will of the Father, and His selfless service to needy humanity. Sister Eva Friedenshort said: "Christ does not bring us into a position where it is impossible to sin, but where it is possible not to sin. Sin in the case of a true believer should be only analogous to a railway accident, and never according to the timetable."

Holy Father, we do hunger and thirst after righteousness. Cleanse us from all evil of thought and word and deed. We ask it in Jesus' name. Amen.

Are you neglecting the storehouse of experience?

Thy testimonies have I taken as an heritage for ever: for they are the rejoicing of my heart. (Psalms 119:111)

A young Christian, packing his bag for a journey, said to a friend, "I have nearly finished packing. All I have yet to put in the bag are a guide book, a lamp, a mirror, a microscope, a telescope, a volume of fine poetry, a few biographies, a package of old letters, a book of songs, a sword, a hammer, and a set of books I have been studying." "But you can't put all that into your bag," objected the friend. "Oh, yes," said the Christian, "here it is," and he placed his Bible in the corner of the suitcase and closed down the lid.

Teach us, O Jehovah, to enrich our lives daily with the vast resources of Thy Scriptures. Amen.

Are you staying too close to the ground?

Now when he had left speaking, he said unto Simon, Launch out into the deep, and let down your nets for a draught. (Luke 5:4)

A mother warned her son, who was entering the Air Corps, "Son, fly low and slow." It was foolish advice. Aviation requires speed and altitude for safety. There must be complete renunciation of the earth for the sky, or tragedy may result. Just so, the Christian life requires a clean break with earthbound thinking, and a complete committal to that which is heavenly. Life is an unproductive affair for many Christians because they are clinging too close to shore; they have not launched "out into the deep" at the word of the Master.

Master, forgive us for toiling fruitlessly in the shallows of life. Give us faith to launch out into the deep at Thy word, for we ask it in Jesus' name. Amen.

Brave hearts know no boundaries, if need is there.

Go ye therefore, and teach all nations . . . (Matthew 28:19)

David Livingstone, who was born at Blantyre, Scotland, 139 years ago, became one of the world's greatest missionaries and explorers. He did more than any other man to combat the slave trade in Africa, to chart its vast geography, and carry the light of Christ to its peoples. He turned his back on wealth and fame in England to stick to his task till his death. When his body was buried in Westminster Abbey in 1874, these lines by an unknown author appeared in *Punch:* "Open the Abbey doors and bear him in to sleep with kings and statesmen, chief and sage. The missionary come of weaver kin, but great by work that brooks no lower wage."

O Thou who didst say, "Go . . . and I am with you alway," comfort, empower, and keep all who are Thy messengers of peace anywhere in the world today. Amen.

It takes all our lights to conquer the darkness.

For with thee is the fountain of life: in thy light shall we see light. (Psalms 36:9)

A little church in Switzerland, according to an old story, had no lighting equipment. So when the villagers wanted to have a service after dark it was necessary for each to carry his own light. It was a pretty sight when they all got together, and when there was a large congregation the lights were very bright. Each one who attended the service made the room a little brighter for the other worshipers, and so the presence of each one helped the light of the church shine a little stronger down the dark valley.

Father of Light, keep us reminded that our lights are not only for our own guidance, but to brighten the way for others. Amen.

Are you trying to shrug off church-going?

. . . as his custom was, he went into the synagogue on the Sabbath day, and stood up for to read. (Luke 4:16)

The Bishop of Exeter asked a man who had come to consult him about personal problems, "Why don't you go to church?" The visitor dismissed the suggestion with the simple statement, "I've been." However, the value of church attendance cannot be learned from a single visit or even occasional attendance. Luke not only tells us that Jesus visited the synagogue in His home town, but that it was His custom to do so. Our souls need regular habits of worship.

We thank Thee, Father, for Thy Church. Help us not only to visit regularly, but to make true worship a habit. Amen.

What Franklin Roosevelt said about missions.

> How beautiful upon the mountains are the feet of him that
> bringeth good tidings, that publisheth peace . . . (Isaiah
> 52:7)

In an interview with Dr. Edgar DeWitt Jones, the late President Franklin D. Roosevelt, said: "Since becoming President I have come to know that the finest types of Americans we have abroad are the missionaries of the Cross. I am humiliated that I am just finding out at this late day the worth of foreign missions and the nobility of the missionaries. Their testimony in China, for instance, during the war there, is beyond praise; their courage thrilling; their fortitude heroic." Wendell Willkie placed the missionaries at the head of the list of creators of good will for America.

O Thou who didst call them to go, give effectiveness to the witness of Thy missionaries around the world, and hasten the coming of Thy kingdom. Amen.

And if from the dream your purpose swerves.

> Turn, O backsliding children, saith the Lord; for I am married unto you: . . . and I will bring you to Zion. (Jeremiah 3:14)

Christian faith is not a ticket on a Pullman train to glory nor an insurance policy against fire in the next world. It is a goal beyond this life and available power to attain it. The goal is to be in perfect fellowship with Christ because we are in perfect harmony with His spirit. We are to share His assurance of immortality, His childlike confidence in the Father, His compassion for mankind, His selfless dedication to its redemption. Paul confessed frankly that he was far from attaining that goal, but asserted: "I press toward the mark for the prize of the high calling of God in Christ Jesus."

Dear God and Father of Jesus Christ, who in Him hast set before us the goal of perfection, keep us from ever being content with a lesser aim. Amen.

The peace that comes from courage in hardship.

> Come unto me, all ye that labour and are heavy laden, and I will give you rest. (Matthew 11:28)

Jesus invites us. But what follows? "Take my yoke upon you,

and learn of me." The call to discipleship is not to snuggle up on a soft and tender breast, but rather to take up a rough cross and walk after a man who climbed a hill and died. He comforted the afflicted, not with opiates, but with strength to take up a bed and walk. He soothed sinners, not by saying that sin did not matter, but with the warning, "Go and sin no more." His rest is not to recline on a couch, but to have strength to carry burdens. His peace is not to hide in a cave, but to enter the battle with undivided heart on the side of right.

Our loving Father, Thou knowest our weakness wants a soft, voluptuous peace. Give us the peace of being brave and the comfort of being strong. We ask this in Jesus' name. Amen.

What religion needs is more demonstrators.

> Take heed unto thyself, and unto the doctrine; continue in them: for in doing this thou shalt both save thyself, and them that hear thee. (I Timothy 4:16)

Paul was concerned that young Timothy should be a good teacher, but first of all that he should be a good man. "Take heed to thyself," he urged, reminding his young friend of the need to live the doctrine, and added, "for in doing this thou shalt both save thyself, and them that hear thee." Arthur Guiterman said it like this: "No printed word nor spoken plea can teach young hearts what men should be; not all the books on all the shelves, but what the teachers are, themselves." Words are handy tools to explain a demonstration, but they are no substitute for the demonstration.

Help us, O Father, in some humble measure to repeat the miracle of the incarnation, as the Word again becomes flesh and walks the earth in our bodies. We ask it in Jesus' name. Amen.

A place to turn your thoughts toward the everlasting.

> And the Lord . . . said unto him, I have heard thy prayer, and have chosen this place to myself for an house of sacrifice. . . .
> Now mine eyes shall be open, and mine ears attent unto the prayer that is made in this place. (II Chronicles 7:12, 15)

We respond to our surroundings. We sense the stimulation of a theatrical atmosphere, or have our nervous tension eased in the quiet tranquillity of home. So a place that is planned for worship and dedicated to God makes it easier for us to be conscious of our Maker. When Solomon dedicated the temple, God told him: "I . . . have chosen this place to myself for an house of sacrifice . . . mine eyes shall be open, and mine ears attent unto the prayer that is made in this place." Every life program ought to include regular worship in a church.

We thank Thee, Father, for freedom of worship, and for the houses dedicated to Thee. We pray Thy blessing upon all who gather in Thy name today. Amen.

You are moved, yes, but to do what?

> Therefore whosoever heareth these sayings of mine, and doeth them, I will liken him unto a wise man, which built his house upon a rock. (Matthew 7:24)

On hearing a gospel sermon we usually approve and agree with what the preacher says. We may compliment him on a well-prepared and helpful discourse, and so feel that our duty is done. Anxious that His hearers not let themselves off so easily, Jesus concluded His Sermon on the Mount with the following: "Therefore whosoever heareth these sayings of mine, and doeth them, I will liken him unto a wise man, which built his house upon a rock." Bishop Massillon, the great French preacher, used to say: "I do not want people to leave my church saying, 'What a wonderful sermon—what a wonderful preacher.' I want them to go out saying, 'I will do something.' "

Grant, Lord, that the sermon we hear today may move us not only to feel deeply, but to act nobly. For Jesus' sake. Amen.

There's challenge in a difficult task.

> Whereupon the king took counsel, and made two calves of gold, and said unto them, It is too much for you to go up to Jerusalem: behold thy gods, O Israel, which brought thee up out of the land of Egypt. (I Kings 12:28)

After dividing the kingdom, Jeroboam feared that Israel would return to allegiance to Jerusalem if the people continued to worship at Dan and Bethel, and announced: "It is too much for you to go up to Jerusalem: behold thy gods . . ." As frequently happens, the multitudes followed the man who would make religion easy for them. To make religion easy, he had to change their gods and thus shunt the people out of the stream of redemption. But an easy religion is powerless. By contrast, Jesus challenges to heroism: "If any man will come after me, let him deny himself, and take up his cross, and follow me."

~ Our good Father, Thou knowest how prone we are to see always the easy way. Strengthen our resolve to follow Christ at any cost. We ask it in His name. Amen.

We will serve God, pay or no pay.

> . . . be it known unto thee, O king, that we will not serve thy gods, nor worship the golden image which thou hast set up. (Daniel 3:18)

The heathen king demanded of the three young Hebrew men: "Is it true . . . do not ye serve my gods, nor worship the golden image which I have set up? Now if ye . . . fall down and worship the image . . . well: but if ye worship not, ye shall be cast the same hour into the midst of a burning fiery furnace; and who is that God that shall deliver you out of my hands?" Their answer: "Our God . . . is able to deliver us . . . out of thine hand, O king. But if not . . . we will not serve thy gods . . ." People say: It pays to serve God. These youths said: We serve God, pay or no pay. Our loyalty is unconditional!

~ God of our fathers, help us to be true to the right because it is right, and not because it is to our advantage. Amen.

THE WAY TO HAPPINESS

The certain path to happiness:

> Not purloining, but shewing all good fidelity; that they may adorn the doctrine of God our Saviour in all things. (Titus 2:10)

A Quaker woman with a beautiful complexion was asked what kind of cosmetic she used. She replied: "I use for my lips, truth; for my voice, prayer; for my eyes, pity; for my hands, charity; for my figure, uprightness; for my heart, love." Paul taught that Christians ought so to live that their lives would make the doctrines of God lovely.

In a world where there is so much ugliness, we thank Thee, God of all beauty, for those whose lives reveal the beauty of Thy teachings. Amen.

Happiness comes from the inside out.

> Then he said unto them, Go your way, eat the fat, and drink the sweet, and send portions unto them for whom nothing is prepared: for this day is holy unto our Lord: neither be ye sorry; for the joy of the Lord is your strength. (Nehemiah 8:10)

The first word of the Sermon on the Mount, "blessed," is sometimes translated "happy." It refers not to fortunate circumstances nor momentary exhilaration, but to the inner state of those who are right at the center of their being. Jesus had a profound joy which gave Him strength to endure the cross. He prayed that we might share it, for joyous Christians are strong Christians. Nehemiah had told his people many years before: "The joy of the Lord is your strength."

Blessed God, we have sometimes allowed self-centeredness, worry, and boredom to destroy our joy. Give us a quality of spirit in which such things cannot exist. Amen.

Do you know when to say no?

> Then said Jesus unto his disciples, If any man will come after me, let him deny himself, and take up his cross, and follow me. (Matthew 16:24)

Horace Mann said: "In vain do they talk of happiness who never subdued an impulse in obedience to principle." Eldon

Roark has been quoted often as telling of the old Negro man saying of his "mistiss" who had brought him up: "She larned me sump'n a man oughta larn early in life—she larned me to don't." Jesus required that those who would follow Him must deny themselves. No one matures mentally, emotionally, or spiritually without learning to deny himself some things in order to procure a higher good.

❧ *Give us wisdom and self-control, O God, to deny ourselves immediate pleasures in order to reach higher goals. Amen.*

Is your life becoming fuller, or emptier?

> But whosoever drinketh of the water that I shall give him shall never thirst; but the water that I shall give him shall be in him a well of water springing up into everlasting life. (John 4:14)

Earth's fountains, like Jacob's well, give momentary refreshment, but not permanent satisfaction. Pleasure, gain, and sin not only require constantly increased draughts from their springs to satisfy, but, by being increased, the satisfaction diminishes. Jesus told the Samaritan woman, who had gone from one companion to another seeking happiness, and who came daily to the well for water: "Whosoever drinketh of the water that I shall give him shall never thirst." When He possesses our hearts, life becomes a matter of increasing fullness, rather than of growing emptiness.

❧ *O Thou who art the living water, grant us to satisfy our thirst from the fountains of Thy grace, and save us from the desire to drink from earth's polluted pools. Amen.*

A rich merchant and his poor son.

> Again, the kingdom of heaven is like unto treasure hid in a field; the which when a man hath found, he hideth, and for joy thereof goeth and selleth all that he hath, and buyeth that field. (Matthew 13:44)

Francis of Assisi was the son of a prosperous merchant, who was proud of him and generous with him. Talented, popular, prosperous, he should have been happy, but he was not. Then, when he stripped off his gay robes and espoused the Lady of Poverty, his father turned from him in bitterness, and his friends forsook him. And lo! The new Francis preached joyously to his brothers the birds, sang the "Canticle of the Sun," and became more jolly than in the days of his youthful hilarity. Others soon began to join him in his poverty, his joyousness, and his delight in God's wonderful world of nature.

Our Father, remembering the words of St. Francis, we would praise Thee, and bless Thee, and give thanks unto Thee, and serve Thee with great humility. Teach us the way of true blessedness. Amen.

A poor king and a rich convict.

O give thanks unto the Lord, for he is good: for his mercy endureth for ever. (Psalms 107:1)

Fabulously rich King Ahab "laid him down on his bed, and turned away his face, and would eat no bread," because Naboth would not sell him his vineyard for an herb garden. But from a Roman prison, Paul could write to friends in Philippi, where he had been stoned: "I have all, and abound: I am full." Gratitude springs from the heart, not from the circumstances. Every life is filled with so many blessings from God that the differences are like the variations in the height of wavelets onthe surface of a bottomless sea. Ingratitude accepts all as but is due, while the thankful heart praises God for even His most austere providence.

O Thou who givest to all liberally and upbraidest not, make us to have the lovely grace of gratitude for all Thy bounteous goodness to us. For Jesus' sake. Amen.

How one man found genuine satisfaction.

When thou shalt besiege a city a long time . . . thou shalt not destroy the trees thereof . . . for the tree of the field is man's life . . . (Deuteronomy 20:19)

One of the busiest men in America recently declared: 'For forty-seven years I have planted at least one tree every year." He is still planting them. Though he no longer expects to see them grow tall, he does hope that someone will be blessed by their shade and beauty and fruit. As he goes about his city and sees the trees of all ages and sizes that he has planted, he has a satisfying sense of having helped God to make His world a little better.

Father, we thank Thee that Thou dost make living things to grow. Teach us to sow faithfully the good and wait patiently for its growth. Amen.

If only I had a million dollars!

Not that I speak in respect of want for I have learned, in whatsoever state I am, therewith to be content. (Phillippians 4:11)

The writer was in prison. He had been whipped, stoned, ship-wrecked, half starved., Yet he professed to be able to take all with unruffled calm and quiet contentment. The secret of his contentment was his discontent. He yearned for a more per-fect union with Christ. He wept for the lost, and would have been willing to be accursed for his Jewish kinsman, He ago-nized in prayer for the work of the churches. Precisely because his craft was loaded with weighty cargo, it was not disturbed with the little waves of material circumstance.

O Thou who art at once the God of peace and of battles, teach us to believe that our God will supply every need, and to know that we can do all things through Christ, for we ask it in His name. Amen.

Are you constantly wondering what people will think?

The Son of man is come eating and drinking . . . Behold a gluttonous man, and a winebibber, a friend of publicans and sinners! (Luke 7:34)

The man who was so welcome in the Bethany home, who took little children in His arms, and who was called by his critics "a gluttonous man, and a winebibber, a friend of publicans and sinners," must have been friendly, sociable and cheerful. People who would have been terribly uncomfortable in the presence of priests and rabbis flocked to Him. No wonder He ws rejected by those whose conception of a religious person was a loud-praying, long-face, officious Pharisee. The warm friendliness and gentle sense of humor of Jesus shocked some but refreshed a great many more.

Dear Master, make us more concerned for the happiness of others than for conformity with conventions. Amen.

Your happiness is within, not without.

Be not hasty in thy spirit to be angry: for anger resteth in the bosom of fools.(Ecclesiastes 7:9)

The Beautitudes, with which Jesus began His Sermon on the Mount, remind us that true blessedness is within ourselves and not in our circumstances. Humble, kind, unselfish people are happy, while proud, malicious, and self-centered people punish themselves, In replying to a letter enclosing some savagely sarcastic verses calling him murderer! coward! liar! Winston Churchill wrote: "I am very sorry to receive your distress of mind. The fact that you do me the greatest injustice does not deprive you of my sympathy since you have obviously suffered so much."

God of peace, dwell Thou within our hearts and by Thy presence create within us the attitudes that make for peace. Amen.

Get the habit of happiness!

Rejoice in the Lord alway. . . (Phillippians 4:4)

Dr. Frank Crane says: "Get the habit! For happiness is largely a matter of habit. Abe Lincoln hit the nail on the head with his usual accuracy, when he said: 'I have noticed that folks are generally about as happy as thay have make up their minds to be!' Many are happy under distressing conditions and many others are wretched though full of food and all dressed up It's habit. Religion ought ot produce happiness." It does when it fills life with meaning by bringing it into harmony with the divine will.

Blessed God, the fullness of whose presence in our hearts brings abundance of joy, fill us with Thy spirit so that an overflow may bless those around us. Amen.

The only people who will ever be really happy.

And now come I to thee; and these things I speak in the world, that they might have my joy fulfilled in themselves. (John 17:13)

Having spent His years doing good, and on the eve of the sacrifice of His life for others, Jesus prayed that His disciples might have His joy fulfilled in themselves. Dr. Albert Schweitzer said to a group of students: I don't know what your destiny will be, but one thing I know: The only ones among you who will be really happy are those who will have sought and found how to serve." On his visit to America he said in answer to a question: "I have found a place of service; that is enough for anyone."

Give us this day, good Father, a share of Thy joy in blessing Thy children. For Jesus' sake. Amen.

CHRISTIAN HERALD ASSOCIATION AND ITS MINISTRIES

CHRISTIAN HERALD ASSOCIATION, founded in 1878, publishes The Christian Herald Magazine, one of the leading interdenominational religious monthlies in America. Through its wide circulation, it brings inspiring articles and the latest news of religious developments to many families. From the magazine's pages came the initiative for CHRISTIAN HERALD CHILDREN'S HOME and THE BOWERY MISSION, two individually supported not-for-profit corporations.

CHRISTIAN HERALD CHILDREN'S HOME, established in 1894, is the name for a unique and dynamic ministry to disadvantaged children, offering hope and opportunities which would not otherwise be available for reasons of poverty and neglect. The goal is to develop each child's potential and to demonstrate Christian compassion and understanding to children in need.

Mont Lawn is a permanent camp located in Bushkill, Pennsylvania. It is the focal point of a ministry which provides a healthful "vacation with a purpose" to children who without it would be confined to the streets of the city. Up to 1000 children between the ages of 7 and 11 come to Mont Lawn each year.

Christian Herald Children's Home maintains year-round contact with children by means of an *In-City Youth Ministry*. Central to its philosophy is the belief that only through sustained relationships and demonstrated concern can individual lives be truly enriched. Special emphasis is on individual guidance, spiritual and family counseling and tutoring. This follow-up ministry to inner-city children culminates for many in financial assistance toward higher education and career counseling.

THE BOWERY MISSION, located at 227 Bowery, New York City, has since 1879 been reaching out to the lost men on the Bowery, offering them what could be their last chance to rebuild their lives. Every man is fed, clothed and ministered to. Countless numbers have entered the 90-day residential rehabilitation program at the Bowery Mission. A concentrated ministry of counseling, medical care, nutrition therapy, Bible study and Gospel services awakens a man to spiritual renewal within himself.

These ministries are supported solely by the voluntary contributions of individuals and by legacies and bequests. Contributions are tax deductible. Checks should be made out either to CHRISTIAN HERALD CHILDREN'S HOME or to THE BOWERY MISSION.

Administrative Office: 40 Overlook Drive, Chappaqua, New York 1051
Telephone: (914) 769-9000